Make an Impact
with your
Written English

Better
Business
English

Make an Impact with your Written English

How to use word power to impress in
presentations, reports, PR and meetings

Fiona Talbot

KOGAN
PAGE

London and Philadelphia

Publisher's note
Every possible effort has been made to ensure that the information contained in this book is accurate at the time of going to press, and the publishers and author cannot accept responsibility for any errors or omissions, however caused. No responsibility for loss or damage occasioned to any person acting, or refraining from action, as a result of the material in this publication can be accepted by the editor, the publisher or the author.

First published in Great Britain and the United States in 2009 by Kogan Page Limited

120 Pentonville Road
London N1 9JN
United Kingdom
www.koganpage.com

525 South 4th Street, #241
Philadelphia PA 19147
USA

© Fiona Talbot, 2009

The right of Fiona Talbot to be identified as the author of this work has been asserted by her in accordance with the Copyright, Designs and Patents Act 1988.

ISBN 978 0 7494 5519 4

British Library Cataloguing-in-Publication Data

A CIP record for this book is available from the British Library.

Library of Congress Cataloging-in-Publication Data

Talbot, Fiona.
  Make an impact with your written English : how to use word power to impress in presentations, reports, PR and meetings / Fiona Talbot.
    p. cm.
  Includes bibliographical references.
  ISBN 978-0-7494-5519-4
  1. English language--Business English--Study and teaching. 2. Business communication. 3. Business writing. I. Title.
  PE1479.B87T355 2009
  808'.06665--dc22
                                        2009017051

Typeset by JS Typesetting Ltd, Porthcawl, Mid Glamorgan
Printed and bound in India by Replika Press Pvt Ltd

Dedication

I would like to thank my family, friends and clients for their support throughout my career. It is a wonderful fact that, by sharing experiences and lessons learnt, we all learn from each other, to our mutual benefit.

Special thanks must go to my dear husband, Colin. I would like to dedicate this series to him – and to my son, Alexander, and my daughter, Hannah-Maria. And to my mother, Lima.

Contents

Preface

How this series works – and what it is about

There are three books in the series, designed to improve your confidence and competence in writing English for global business. They are designed on three levels, to fit in with the three stages in the business cycle.

My central philosophy is this: writing business English effectively for international trade is about creating clear, concise messages and avoiding verbosity. But the fewer words you write, the more important it is that you get them right.

Book 1: How to Write Effective Business English

This book assumes that you know English to intermediate level and provides effective guidelines. It deals with real-life scenarios, to give you answers that even your boss may not know.

It uses a system that also gives you the building blocks to take you to the next level in the cycle of success, set out in Book 2.

Book 2: Make an Impact with your Written English

This book will take you a further step forward in your executive career.

You will learn how to use written word power to promote and sell your messages, as well as 'brand you'. You will learn how to make your mark writing English, whether for PR, presentations, reports, meeting notes, manuals etc. And for cyberspace, where English is today's predominant language.

You will learn how to deal with pressing challenges that you need to be aware of. And how to write English that impresses, so that you get noticed for the right reasons.

Book 3: Executive Writing Skills for Managers

This book deals with the English business writing you need at the top of your career and focuses on writing as a key business tool.

It gives amazingly valuable tips on harmonizing the English that you and your teams use (for example, for evaluation performance) – tips that you quite simply have not seen before. It also introduces the concept of Word Power Skills 2.0 – for unified English business writing that keeps everyone in the loop.

The importance of business English today

Increasingly, English language is the language of choice used in multinational gatherings. It may not be the predominant language of the group, but is the most likely to be understood by the majority – at least at a basic level – so becomes a powerful tool for communication and inclusion.

You may have to unlearn some things you learnt at school

Writing English for business today is highly unlikely to be the same as the writing you were taught at school or university. Apart from getting your punctuation and grammar right, the similarities often end there.

This series works with the business cycle

The series highlights the essential role business writing plays at every stage in your career path – and alongside the cycle of business in general. Figures 1 and 2 show how this works. I describe below how it relates to the three phases.

Phase one: joining an organization or setting up your own business

English business writing needs at the outset of your career: a CV, letter, job application, start-up plan or business plan, routine business writing tasks.

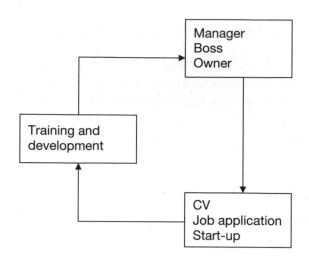

Figure 1 The business cycle: from the individual's perspective

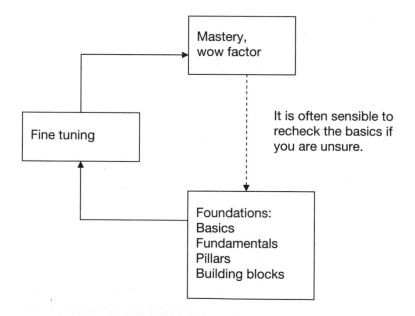

Figure 2 The business cycle: from the business writing perspective

As you start your career, you need to understand how to get the basics right. You need to understand how to write correctly, how spelling, punctuation and grammar matter. You will not get to the next phase in your career – the pitching phase – without getting the basics right.

Phase two: you develop through knowing how to harness word power

Your developing English business writing needs; making impact in everything you write in English; personal self-development or other training.

Great business English writing will generate ideas and sparks that capture readers' attention and take your career forward. Powerful writing can sell your proposals so well – weak writing can do the exact opposite.

Phase three: mastery of written word power enables you to shine and lead

English business writing needs at the height of your career: mastery of written word power required for leadership, to shine as a manager, boss and/or owner.

You do not get to the top by blending in. You have to build bridges, shape outcomes and lead through word power. You need to express your ideas in writing – so use business English that makes readers want to buy in.

The series is an easy, indispensable, comprehensive guide

It is an essential tool kit to keep by your desk or take on your travels. Dip in and out of it as and when you need the answers it provides, to help you shine in all stages of your career.

So each of the three books aligns with the business cycle and supports your development and perfection of writing English for business to gain the competitive edge – because the development of the written word goes hand in hand with, or even is, the business cycle itself.

Get results!

Just take a look at my methods, focus on the elements that apply to your business writing and make sure they become an intrinsic part of your real-life performance.

This series does not take you away from your job; it focuses on your job and uses word power as a free resource. All you have to do is harness this – and enjoy the benefits of immediate results and sustainable improvements.

Good luck on your journey to success!

Fiona Talbot
TQI Word Power Skills
www.wordpowerskills.com

Introduction

By the end of this book, you will know how to write business English from your readers' perspective, so that your words say what you mean them to say!

You will know how to succeed in writing English with the right impact for your target cross-cultural audience, how to sell your messages and promote your organization – and how to make your mark through 'brand you'!

1

Writing English for business

Defining readers, customers and audience

Throughout this book I use the terms readers, target readership, customers and audience interchangeably. I use 'customer' both in its most common usage as a person who buys goods or services from a business, and in the broadest sense of signifying a person that you deal with in the course of your daily work. So the term applies just as much to internal colleagues, suppliers, those in charities or the public sector etc as it does to those who are external buying consumers.

Your audience can be anyone and everyone

I use many practical examples and scenarios in this book that relate to standard sales or customer pitches. Because we are all consumers in our private lives, we can easily relate to and understand these examples. What I would like to stress is that the concepts apply equally to every scenario in the list that follows. Think of lobbying; think of politics; think of charities; think of fundraising; think of promotions.

Different cultures, different approaches

The 'standard English' I use throughout this book is likely to be understood by users of the other varieties of English that I will be describing. The list of these varieties is extensive; to give you an idea I will just mention UK or British English, Australian English, US English and Caribbean English.

So what is meant by 'standard English'? For the purposes of this book I use the expression to mean the English routinely described in mainstream UK English dictionaries and grammar books.

How do I define business English? English is a major international language of commercial communication. It is also the language of the internet and of global access to knowledge. Business English is quite simply the name given to the English used for dealing with business communication in English.

When I write in this book about 'native English speakers', I mean anyone who speaks any variety of English as their first language. Non-native English speakers may learn English in any of the following categories: English as a foreign language

(EFL), English for speakers of other languages (ESOL) and English as an acquired language (EAL), all self-explanatory terms; and English as a second language (ESL). In the ESL category, learners are likely to be in a setting where the main or official language is English but their native tongue is not. It can be a confusing term when used to describe someone who is actually learning English as a third or fourth language, as can be the case.

There is some debate within academic circles as to which of these terms (or others) should be used. As this is not an academic but a business-oriented book, I choose to use a different convention here. Throughout the book you will find that I use:

- the term native English (NE) speaker or writer to denote a person whose first language is English, and native English (NE) writing to refer to their writing;

- the term non-native English (non-NE) speaker or writer to denote a person whose first language is not English, and non-native English (non-NE) writing to refer to their writing.

Approaching that white space

During my Word Power workshops I ask attendees to think about writing on a topic of their choice, something about which they are very knowledgeable, on just one side of a sheet of A4 paper. They have that blank sheet in front of them and before they start I ask, 'How much of that space do you think your writing will fill?'

Before they answer, I already have a fair idea of responses I am likely to receive from different cultures. You might think the answers will be totally personality-driven. But the way we write can also be culture-driven, at least at the outset of our writing careers. As an illustration, compare your own response with what I have found to be a typical British response.

By their own admission, when the British write for business, they generally tend to feel that it is an obligation to 'fill all the white space' with writing. This may seem strange as there is a very strong move in the UK to embrace plain English and concise messages. But this is a relatively new development and writers can have an instinctive (though false) feeling that readers might actually feel short-changed by brevity. This false premise can lead to writers overcompensating: writing too much information, without making an effort to prioritize key facts and edit out overload. Unfortunately, writing waffle comes easily to the native English writer. Even when they know it is far from ideal, it can be a bad habit that is difficult to discard. To be fair, the British are certainly not alone: many other cultures favour verbosity too.

In sharp contrast, some nationalities and cultures have a totally opposite approach. When faced with that blank piece of paper, they decide that the best way forward is to leave as much white space unfilled as they possibly can. They write short bullet points, short lists, and maybe add a diagram. There you are, they think, the job is done. But is it? Are such writers always really as efficient as they think? Do they ever realize that their writing may not actually work? The real proof can be in readers' reactions and subsequent action (or inaction).

Great writing is certainly as concise as it needs to be, but it does not cut the intended and correct meanings out. Nor should it remove the right words to create logical connections to and for readers. Great business writers know when to amplify, with words that add value, and when to edit down, when to cut out the waffle. It is about understanding what needs to be expressed rather than implied and what is not needed at any given time.

Just because we know what our shorthand and our stark bullet points mean, it does not necessarily follow that our readers do too. If we fall into the trap of excessive brevity, this is just as bad as the trap of verbosity and waffle. In both cases, we take our readers into a world of customer disservice. Readers of any nationality will not thank us for that. To demonstrate, let's compare two rather extreme styles of writing. First example:

> The head of department reported that the additional, unexpectedly inflated, expenditure on office stationery, arising from the company rebranding exercise, could not be met from current reserves and that, although he might have to ask staff to make savings, it did appear that the expenditure could be accommodated by putting an embargo on any managers undertaking any first-class travel in December.

The length of the sentence and the number of commas needed show that the sentence needs editing. All the reader really needs to know is that:

■ there is additional, unexpected expenditure that cannot be met from current reserves;

■ a ban on first-class travel in December would recoup this amount;

■ if not, staff might have to be asked to make savings.

Here is the second example:

■ Absenteeism;

■ Stocking shelves;

■ Waste.

In the second example, a bullet-point list, only the writer knows what they mean. Even if it is going to be explained face to face at some stage, this writing is never going to be meaningful. Yet just a small amount of reworking would make it meaningful. For example, maybe 'Absenteeism' in the first bullet point means: 'problem of absenteeism; solutions needed'. The subject immediately becomes more accessible and means more to readers, even before discussion.

Which of the two examples is your style closer to? Is either extreme ideal? When you write for global business it is generally going to work better to go for a middle path. Develop a style that certainly edits down to the main points (cutting out waffle) but also includes enough information, so that every message is entire and meaningful. It is crucial you do this in your writing. Writing is a medium that is likely to be read when you are not there to explain it – and which may also be relayed to recipients of whom you may be unaware.

Different cultures, different personalities

It can help readers to know, in the broadest terms, what a particular non-NE writer's background is. That writer's choice of words and the way they write is likely to reflect this. Armed with some awareness of this, readers are more likely to allow some leeway in interpretation – and be more tolerant. It can make all the difference; and it can provide 'Eureka' moments, in which readers are more likely to see why the writer wrote in a particular way.

I will shortly use examples from 'Dutch-English' to illustrate this point. To put things in perspective, the Dutch can be some of the best business English writers in the world. They get their English right, more than they get it wrong. A proud nation of traders, they accept that Dutch is not a global language and that they need to master other languages to succeed in international trade. Yet even they routinely make the same mistakes when they write in English. Although these may be small mistakes, they can confuse native and non-native English readers unaccustomed to these idiosyncrasies. Here are some examples:

The Dutch translation of the English word 'or' is 'of'. So Dutch-English will regularly include errors such as 'either you of Gert could go to the meeting' (correct English: 'either you or Gert could go to the meeting').

Another common mistake is to use 'or ... or' in English instead of 'either ... or'. For example: 'or we go to London or we go to Paris' (correct English: 'either we go to London or we go to Paris').

These errors seem minor but they really can make life difficult for readers. If, however, readers understand that these are errors that the Dutch (as one example) often make, it helps them to understand the correct meaning.

Understanding personality alongside culture can also be helpful. Some personalities tend to write the waffle that takes readers all over the place rather than where they want to be.

When readers know a writer's background, they are likely to be:

■ less offended by extremely direct exchanges;

■ less puzzled by deferential language where people do not appear willing to take the lead on decisions;

■ less frustrated by hierarchical language where a writer will only deal with a chief executive;

■ less impatient with writing by consensus where the individual is not empowered to respond;

■ less bemused by overly polite language.

Your checklist for action

■ See writing as a fundamental skill for you as an individual and for your business.

■ Develop and improve your business English writing at every opportunity throughout your career.

■ Remember that business writing in its many forms is your most common route to market. Be the best.

■ Consider cross-cultural socializing and networking, or formal company training in how to succeed in international business. You will learn much that will help you know how to write the right business English for your target audience.

2

Deciding your business writing objectives

Describing what you and your organization do

There is a three-way relationship between you and your business writing:

■ First of all you need to know how to describe what you do.

■ Second, you need to know how to describe this within the framework of what your organization does.

■ Third, you must identify what you need to achieve each time you write.

It sounds like common sense, yet people do not always take the time to think this through. That is why I make a point of asking this question: why are you writing English for business? In my training workshops, attendees generally answer this by listing the following aims:

■   to inform or record;

■   to seek information;

■   to write specifications;

■   to achieve a standard;

■   to write reports.

They then come to a halt – even when sales and marketing teams are involved. I always have to quiz them: surely there are other reasons? After some head scratching and soul searching, some then manage to list the aims I am really looking for, namely:

■   to persuade;

■   to promote services;

■   to engage interest and involve;

■   to get the right results;

■   to sell;

■   to support customers;

■   to improve life for our customers;

■   to eat, breathe and live our vision.

Interestingly and encouragingly, that last point, 'to eat, breathe and live our vision', was made by a relatively junior employee working for a charity. The workshop she was attending was an open one, and the majority of delegates were from the private sector. She made the point with such sincerity and conviction that she absolutely wowed everyone else.

Surely words that wow should be uppermost in our minds when we write? If we hide the most important words and aims in the back of our mind, how can we ever write with impact? And why would we ever be motivated to bother?

I am going to show you a writing system in Chapter 7 that will help you design great written English for business. But it will not work nearly so well if you do not first look at where you fit into the picture.

Focus on the message, not just the translation

If you are a non-native English (non-NE) reader reading in your own language, let me ask you this: do you prefer reading business writing that is clear or complicated, even muddled? By far the majority of non-NE readers will vote for clear business writing. Yet the moment a reader becomes a writer can be the moment when they shift emphasis. It is as if non-NE writers almost worry that they might be too clear. It is as if they think that writing that is easy cannot impress.

Unfortunately, non-NE writers can have a general fear that they will fail when they write English for business. This anxiety can lead to a preoccupation about translating from their language into English, maybe on a word-for-word basis. The irony is that focusing on translating single components can make non-NE writers lose sight of their intrinsic business message. The overall meaning may not be the sum of each individual word, especially if you choose even one wrong word. What you are setting out to achieve gets lost, so your message becomes subordinate to the translation.

English dictionary syndrome

This is probably one of the biggest problems for non-NE speakers. It happens when people turn to a dictionary to find the most complicated-sounding translation of the word they are looking for. It is something that almost everyone does, and it can become a real problem.

If you want to get your translation right, use standard and online dictionaries with the utmost caution. As a rule, go for the simple word in the list rather than the most complicated. You are not going to be seen as uneducated if you choose to write 'wise' instead of 'erudite' or 'many' instead of 'a plethora of'.

The opposite is true: the more complex the expression, the more likely it is that readers will judge your English as pretentious. The irony is that people in business are usually more impressed by simply expressed facts. That is why there is a major shift these days towards plain English in business. This means using simple language wherever possible. So if all the words you find in a dictionary are really unfamiliar, check with someone who really knows English whether they can verify their correct use.

Another risk you run is that you may be seen as condescending (ie showing a feeling of superiority to someone of a 'lower rank'). This can happen if you put someone in the difficult position of having to ask you what your writing means – that is, if they dare or can be bothered. Also, although you may choose 'intelligent-sounding' words from dictionaries, they can seem odd, even funny, to readers in general.

An example is antiquated English terminology that harks back to a bygone era; for example:

'We cherish cooperation with your highly esteemed good selves.'

This sort of language is strangely prevalent in brochures and on websites written in English for global business. If you know your writing needs evaluating, take this opportunity to revisit your words. It will not cost you much. In fact, word power is a virtually free resource that will enhance your business.

Online translations

Online translations can, on occasion, hit the mark. But they can also have a bad effect on business performance. Blind acceptance of online translations can lead users to a false sense of security.

Native speakers can spot the syndrome at a glance. It yields splendidly incorrect offerings such as:

'The industrial area looked to carry off the market this summer.'

'We need assignment professionals with a good eye for the detail.'

I will convert these into 'real' English:

'The manufacturing sector appeared to outperform the market this summer.'

'We need committed professionals with a keen eye for detail.'

You can see what has happened. Some online English translations are actually nonsensical. They may seem to be free, but they will ultimately cost you by sabotaging your communication and therefore your business objectives.

So can you ever justify using online translations? Yes, if you use them with care. Try to use the simplest expressions

– and see if they are really being used in real life business today. Ask an English-speaking colleague or customer. Read current business books and articles; look at major companies' websites in English. Get a feel for what works. You will see for yourself that it is not necessarily the biggest words or the longest sentences and paragraphs that are effective. Good business English is not about what I call 'out-Englishing' or 'over-Englishing' the English. This describes what happens when non-native English writers fail by trying too hard.

Idioms

Nor is good business English about trying too hard by using too many idioms.

An idiom is a phrase or usage peculiar to a language, and it can have a meaning that you may not expect. Never pretend you understand an English idiom if you are not completely sure of it, because it can land you in difficulties. These examples show how you cannot work the meanings of idioms simply from the words themselves:

'A penny for your thoughts' means 'What are you thinking about?'

'To make a mountain out of a molehill' means 'to exaggerate the importance of a problem'.

'A little bird told me' means 'Someone (whom I do not wish to name) told me.'

Also, if you do understand an idiom, do not use it if your target audience might not understand it. The advice works both ways. It can be too high a risk to try to translate an idiom from another language into English. The following example demonstrates this:

'Don't be the piano man. There's no need to hit the keys too hard.'

The example uses two idioms from another language that the non-NE writer translated (incorrectly) into English. Most of his target readership had no idea what he meant; nor do I. Do you?

Here is another example of a foreign idiom translated into English:

'This is pushing me up the palm tree.'

I am told that this means 'This is irritating' – though maybe it means something else. Such uncertainty is a problem, so why make life harder by making people unsure?

'Brand you' and your company brand

The essential step towards total success is to realize that everyone in a company has their own identity. This coexists with, and depends on, the identity of the business for which they work. Ideally an organization should make everybody feel valued. Personal self-development should be encouraged, as should the fact that each person is an ambassador for that company. If all embrace this concept, it becomes clear that every piece of writing you put out, can and should actively market both 'brand you' and your company brand.

You do this by letting people see how, in everything you write, you come over as strongly as your organization. By doing this, you become valuable to your valued reader. Your commitment to making a difference by 'being you' – and seizing the opportunity that 'being you' brings – can yield such positive results. Others in your organization may get poor if their writing is unenthusiastic. In stark contrast, you _____ give your audience the feel-good factor through your own sense of pride, and therefore enthusiasm, about what you do. From the start they will feel warm rather than cold towards your suggestions.

Think about the cycle of business. Think about the value of your business English writing from the point when you apply for a job right through to excelling in that job and achieving promotion – and then throughout your ongoing career.

Incidentally, did you know that if you write down your aspirations you are more likely to achieve them? And what if I said that the right written English could double your chances of getting your dream job? Then I would be wrong. It could actually quadruple your chances. That is how important words are – and how important English is globally.

So let's put word power to work in defining 'brand you'. It may be that you have never thought of yourself as a brand, but you will understand the concept of brand in business. So think of a well-known brand. I will take the example of Coca-Cola, simply because almost everyone has heard of it. Why is it well known? Largely because over years and years of clever global marketing and communication, the company has made you able to identify the product and bring it readily to mind.

Have you ever been part of a branding exercise at work? I am not necessarily talking here about an explicit marketing assignment; it could be creating a new project or a new product launch to end-users. People tend to get passionate about this and give it their all. In fact, that is when people may give their best performance. So with all this in mind, why should it be any different when you are thinking of starting a new job, career or venture? When the brand is you, you should be looking for your personal best. If you realize that you are the benchmark, then everything you do from that point on will be just as good.

Why save your best for someone else? Of course you need to do your best for others too, but become number one in your own sense of self-worth. The best you can be. Identify how you could take the opportunity now of defining 'brand you'.

Do this in writing, and in accessible English. Then write your formula for success and see how you can make it happen. Once you have created your brand, this will give you the confidence to excel at everything you do.

To help you, just think about the words in English that most accurately capture 'brand you'. It is important to be realistic about this and not exaggerate. You have to deliver what you say.

Maybe some of the following words fit the bill:

highly motivated;

enthusiastic;

energized;

hard working;

good communicator;

self-driven;

self-starter;

creative;

team player.

It may help to ask colleagues what words they would use to describe you. They may come up with other suggestions, such as:

high-achiever (perhaps over-achiever);

conscientious;

reliable;

polite;

considerate;

good mediator;

calm under stress;

quality conscious;

totally professional;

pays attention to detail.

Why not make a note now of some English words and phrases that capture what you think best describes 'brand you'?

Understanding the image you should promote at all times is one way in which you can make your mark through the medium of business writing. You may be a Nobel-winning physicist, but if you just have to send one e-mail to a person, that may be all they know about you. So if you write blandly, for example, 'It appears this may have some potential', your readers will most likely perceive you to be bland – even worse, uninteresting and uninterested.

On the other hand, if your English expresses interest and enthusiasm – for example: 'I'm excited by this opportunity'

– you are far more likely to engage their attention and make your mark.

Indeed, once you see this potential for dual marketing (ie of both yourself and of your organization) this can transform your performance. You too can sell, without expressly being part of your company's sales team. Naturally, I'm talking here about implicit selling as opposed to explicit selling. Effective writing should sell personal expertise as well as a company's products and services (by implication at least). After all, when we talk about a consistently professional and quality-conscious workforce, this has to mean everyone, every time.

Let's look at examples of e-mails in English that may sell the writers short. They may feel they are totally professional but their writing suggests otherwise. They may also be quite unaware of the judgement others might make.

The first is a request for information. The following e-mail was sent to an external provider by a company's training manager:

'Hi can you send out a quotation for a training course?'

The recipient's likely perception is that the request could be more professionally presented, not only in terms of layout but also in terms of introducing the writer and their company, and at least outlining likely needs. Also, there is no 'please' or 'thank you', which really need to be expressed in e-mail just as much as in letters.

Next is an example of an interim reply. This update was sent by e-mail to an internal colleague:

'Sorry this is late but I hope you don't mind. Please bare with us while we gather the remaining info.'

Here the recipient's likely initial perception is that there is some empathy here, which is good: at least the writer is sorry that the update is late. But actually, yes, perhaps they do mind that the reply is late, and they may sense that the writer does not really care. In fact, the writer could not be bothered to check their spelling – it should be 'bear', not ' bare' – nor could they manage to write 'information' instead of 'info'. This writing is simply not professional.

Now an example involving the sending of a presentation. This e-mail was sent to an external client:

> 'Please find my presentation attached. I have to tell you at the outset that I haven't had much time to prepare, so there are sure to be mistakes.'

The recipient's likely perception is that they really do not want to see a mistake-riddled piece of work. Do they not deserve first-class attention? No doubt they would have been much happier if the writer had taken more time to prepare and check the quality, even if it meant negotiating a slight extension of time.

How to promote brand you: some examples

There are some business writers who manage to put their imprint on everything they write. Even though, like everyone else, I receive a barrage of e-mail, their messages shine out and make me want to read them. These writers make a difference every time they write.

Here are some e-mail extracts that demonstrate what I mean.

Dear (name)
Spring days, full of summer promise
I hope this e-mail finds you very well indeed.
The winter is over, the spring buds are awakening, so let me now introduce our summer schedule, which is full of good things to look forward to.
(signature)

E-mail disclaimer (part extract)
We have an environmentally friendly e-mail policy and hope you share this with us. When we print an e-mail, we make sure we use recycled paper and we dispose of it responsibly. Please pass the message on!

An ideal solution for your needs
Many thanks for your e-mail and for setting out your precise requirements.
I have pleasure in enclosing what I think you may see as the perfect solution, which has the added benefit of being well within your budget. Of one thing you can be sure: our company is 100% committed to your satisfaction.

Your support appreciated
Very many thanks for your great efforts in coming up with a more affordable and even more helpful solution for our clients.
I greatly appreciate your support and they are going to be delighted!

'Brand you' is what you make it. Nobody else but you can fill in the detail. I cannot tell you how to define your personal brand – but I can encourage you to identify it and not to undermine yourself. Take time to think through the image you wish to present. Link this to the message you also need to project. Then ensure you do this consistently in your memos, e-mails, reports, letters, presentations, website and brochures – in fact, in everything you write in English. I cannot stress enough how this can show both brand you and your company brand (or, in the non-commercial sector, your organization's values) in a good light.

Your checklist for action

- In everything you write in English, focus on the message, not just the translation; don't rely on online translation tools – always review results critically.

- Avoid making your writing over-complicated by choosing difficult English words from dictionaries.

- Recognize that it may be better to avoid idioms when writing English across cultures.

- Identify 'brand you' and how you should project this positively in your writing.

- Promote your company or organization values and your personal brand or values in all your writing.

- Do not sell yourself short: be totally professional at all times.

- Make your mark every time you write in English – and elicit favourable responses based on your own sense of pride about what you do.

3

Reading and writing challenges and needs

Help your readers

It may surprise you to find that even your choice of font or margin layout impact on whether your written English is intrinsically fit for your international target audience. There is a commercial need to address the overall look and legibility of your writing, as this chapter will show.

All readers have needs, whether internal readers within our organization or external readers. Both are likely to have the same concerns when they read business communication. Indeed, whether our writing succeeds or fails depends very much on readers' reactions to the following statements or questions:

■ I like the look and feel of this.

- This is important.

- It is clearly in my interests to read this and/or react to it.

- This is sincere; I like a company to care about my needs and serve me well.

- This is enthusiastic and reasoned; I can buy into this.

- This seems like an organized business that knows what it is writing about.

- I can make an informed decision based on this information.

- I know what to do and when – and it's easy.

- What does this mean?

- I cannot begin to think how to reply to this, so I'll put it to the bottom of my in-tray.

- This is not important.

- This is insincere or grovelling.

- This is badly presented and looks boring.

- This is disjointed. It probably represents the way the company does business.

- There's too much hassle involved to know what to do and whether it's right for me.

- Do I have to do anything or not? I'm too busy, so I will do nothing.

If we now substitute the word 'customers' for 'readers', does this make you want to get each message right first time? I hope so. Try to have the image of a customer in mind when you write anything at all. If things need doing, always give the reasons why.

If you want to get the positive responses in the first half of the list above, then design writing that will achieve this. If necessary, refer to the overall context to help you succeed. If you cannot be bothered to do this, then be prepared for the responses typified by the negatives in the list!

Reading and writing challenges – how writing with impact can help

Almost everyone gets tired when reading large amounts of text, and this is especially true when we read from computer screens. It is a major reason why good writers of web copy break their material into sections and then subdivide these further with headings, subheadings and links. By clicking on the links, readers can access further information as and when they need it. The choice and the timing are theirs.

For some people, reading presents more challenges than for others. Imagine how much more difficult it might be for them to read English if it is not their first language. So write English that everyone has more chance of reading easily. Writing is not just about words. It can be about appearance too.

If you have dyslexia or the visual condition known as Irlen syndrome, to take just two examples, this can alter the way you see the written word, even in your own language. Your eyes may not just tire when reading, you may also find it difficult to read. It may be a problem for you to keep track of words on a line and you may skip words. All the more reason for writers to understand that writing with impact makes practical sense – from all angles.

If you can colour-code information, that can be a great help to readers. If you can research what your readers like, do so. If you know that someone in your target audience is colour-blind, you might want to avoid red and green. Certain coloured paper can help print stand out for certain readers (cream and pale yellow suit many) but a patterned background can make things far worse for others.

Use the tips given throughout this book to understand when to use visuals and visual imagery, pie charts, bar charts, pictograms and numbers (which many readers will find part-icularly useful) alongside your words.

Managers need to be aware that they should support staff that may need help regarding these issues. It all impacts on writing English for business successfully.

Choose the right font for international business

Most of us do not have secretaries or typesetters, but have to do our own business English writing or typing. Even choosing the right font – one that most readers can read – can be essential to getting your business English right and fit for purpose.

Choice of fonts may have to be made on a corporate basis. If not, you may have the chance to make your mark by choosing a reader-friendly font. So what fonts should you choose? Many non-English-speaking companies use Times New Roman for English. This is a very readable font – and readability is certainly important. Some foreign readers would find it difficult to read some other fonts that are routinely used for English. This may be because of the way they scan a page in their own language.

The UK Learning and Skills Council recommends Arial, Times New Roman and Helvetica. Other fonts such as Tahoma and Verdana are favoured by website designers for their readability online. In normal circumstances, it is generally recommended that 12-point size is used for ordinary type and 14-point for headlines. This can be varied according to your target audience and indeed may have to be increased for some readers.

When writing English for websites or leaflets, check whether any legislation applies regarding readability. This can vary from country to country.

But readability is not the only factor. When it comes to writing business English, do you want a readable font for an international arena that readers also perceive as artistic and creative? Or solid and dependable? It may seem strange to write this way about fonts, but readers do have such perceptions. For example:

Comic Sans MS can seem to indicate conversation and can be perceived as friendly.

Times New Roman is definitely readable but can seem old-fashioned these days. Yet this is the font that many countries use as a default font for writing English, without realizing that it may not be appropriate for all.

Verdana was designed as a font for e-writing.

Century Gothic is viewed as artistic, though many complain it is not easy to read.

Arial is chosen by many government offices and learning providers as being easy to read.

Tahoma is also chosen by these users for the same reason.

What do you think about the following font, which I have seen businesses use?

The look and feel of documents are also very important in any book about effective writing. How might your readers or customers feel about reading this, especially if there's a really important message embedded in it? What might happen if you or your colleagues cannot be bothered to set out letters and other documentation the way your readers expect?

If you are a non-native English writer you will have your own difficult-for-foreigners-to-read fonts (maybe antique-style) in your own language. They may work in some areas of your home market. But can you see how difficult to read they may be for foreigners or people who find it difficult to process things visually?

In case you cannot decipher the text in the last box, let me now show you how much easier it is to read in a clear font:

> The look and feel of documents are also very important in any book about effective writing. How might your readers or customers feel about reading this, especially if there's a really important message embedded in it? What might happen if you or your colleagues cannot be bothered to set out letters and other documentation the way your readers expect?

Companies generally use handwriting style fonts where they want to appear 'friendly' and informal and reach out to new markets. There is certainly nothing wrong with that, but there are fonts (such as Comic Sans MS) that will achieve a similar effect and still be readable for most people.

Feedback that I have collected is that the 'spidery' font shown on the previous page comes across as almost unintelligible and un-businesslike. The commercial outcomes can be:

- Although there are times when a jokey font or slogan validly engages readers' attention, it is never good news for readers to view your core business as a joke.

- If your message is so embedded in text that your target readers cannot read it, they may not even be bothered to try.

- Non-NE readers especially may misunderstand your message.

- Any reader may take the wrong action, or no action at all.

- Readers might come back to you for clarification (which costs you and them both time and money).

- They might tell others about you (in a negative way).

So do make an informed choice as to which font is right for your business and your international readers.

A further tip: be aware that much of the design and thought you put in may be lost when sent to an electronic device. This point is especially important if you are likely to send written messages while travelling abroad.

Underlining, italics and justifying margins

There is definitely less underlining in business English writing today – probably mainly as a result of the fact that so much writing is now electronic. Website designers discourage any underlining that does not denote a hyperlink. This is to avoid confusion, as these days we expect underlining on our computer screens to signify a hyperlink. We expect to be able to click on it and be taken immediately to some new information. It puzzles us if this does not happen.

The trouble is, a lot of standard textbooks in English have not kept up with this development and may still show letter or e-mail templates that use underlining. Or you may have been taught to use underlining in report headings and findings.

Italic writing can also be difficult for non-native English readers to read, so use it sparingly in your business English writing.

Before we leave the physical appearance of writing in English, it is worth mentioning that non-native (but also many native) English readers can find it easier to read writing in which the margins are aligned on the left ('left justified') but are ragged on the right of the page. Publishers adopt a different convention, as you see in this book.

Technology of the 'instantly available'

Newcomers to the workforce from the i-generation, the Google generation, or whatever term you choose to use, are increasingly comfortable with the fact that business writing needs to adapt to new technology and conventions.

This means that conventions in business writing are changing. The traditional model for writing that many of us know (from writing English essays or dissertations at school or college) is becoming sidelined. The model that is being ditched is:

beginning;

middle;

end.

Why? Because the flow of the new technology that feeds an 'I want it now' mentality in users is unstoppable. Information in English (especially as this is the predominant language of the web) is more often than not now broken down into bite-sized (and byte-sized!) chunks. Even when a traditionally constructed report is prepared in English, business writers today often highlight the main points in a covering letter, note or e-mail.

Another tip to help you is this. Because of information 'fast-load' and overload, we may not think about things as much as we should. This is when mistakes happen. So if you are a non-native English writer writing in English for business, do factor in extra, not less, time than when you write in your own language.

Scan reading and skimming: a new norm

A really helpful tip is this: understand that today's readers tend to scan read or skim read. They look at written text quickly to identify relevant information and get an overview of contents. It is:

- partly to do with processing information overload;

- partly because reading from computer screens is tiring;

- partly because readers actively want to reduce the number of words they have to read.

Writers cannot ignore the fact that readers will probably make less commitment to read what we write online than on paper. Quite simply, they will give up faster.

Tips to help you are these:

- Scan and skim reading are further evidence that readers are likely to react fairly instantly to the look of writing.

- If they are external readers who are unknown to you, they are likely to ask themselves: 'Do I like this writing? Do I need it? Will it help me better than information from another provider in more accessible English?'

■ They are also likely to consider: 'Will this writing help me now, or do I bookmark it for later?' All the more reason to make initial impact – maybe deliver fuller meaning later in the writing.

■ You can help your written words make this initial impact by choosing simple yet powerful words, great visuals, meaningful topic headings and subheadings; also by reinforcing your messages.

■ Non-native English readers, who may be overwhelmed by language they do not fully understand, can then have the opportunity to focus at the later (revisiting) stage on any words that they may need to look up.

Your checklist for action

■ Today the initial impact of your writing is key. Design it well – to be effective immediately.

■ Take care to choose the right font, other visual devices and layout to help you write English for your international target audience.

■ Consider a house style (that everyone in the organization can reproduce) for a professional look and feel.

■ Be aware that writing is rapidly evolving, especially in business. This is driven by the various online electronic channels now becoming dominant in all our lives.

■ Design your key messages in instantly accessible English so that even in a world of distractions they can be seen and understood at a glance.

4

Writing for presentations and talks

Create an advantage: get noticed for the right reasons

We almost all have to give presentations or talks in business today. There is an irony here though: both can actually be as much about writing as about talking.

Why? Because both usually start out as points captured in writing. And an often overlooked fact is that both usually end in writing too – whether in the shape of a handout at the time or a written follow-up afterwards. That is when your words can be judged by your audience in the cold light of day – when you are not there to explain them. So if you are using English, you better get your written English right!

There is something else you also need to appreciate if you are truly working in English in a global arena. It is that presentations can be the new form of the business report. You may think you are presenting to six people, but your well-written slides may in fact be sent out internationally. People do not listen to the words at that stage; they read them.

In fact, I have clients whose English slides have actually become company mantra. That is how important the writing – not the speech – has become.

Why do any of us give a presentation? Is it for fun? I doubt if anyone would say that. It will almost always be for a clear business purpose. The same goes for your written proposal answering a formal request for information. In fact, a good written proposal can be the key to that first step inside a potential customer's door. It too is writing that may be passed around and judged in your absence.

A presentation is an area where you usually have to deliver very quickly. A company to whom you are pitching for new business may give you 15 minutes maximum. That gives you as little as 10 minutes to pitch and 5 minutes to answer questions. So if you are not to waste your or their time, you must use the time to shine. If you do not go flat-out to ensure that the presentation or talk propels you into your target company's future, why bother to be there? And remember, most presenters run out of time.

This is why great written slides and handouts with the right call to action become invaluable. They can sell for you after you have left.

You can create a position of strength by being a non-native English presenter

Whatever you do, do not get noticed for the wrong reasons. You will be noticed a hundred times more for using the wrong written word than for avoiding it and choosing the simpler English word that everyone understands.

Get the right spotlight on yourself whether you are delivering an internal or external presentation. In terms of quality, why differentiate? A presentation should always be good. Your internal presentation may be for the people who hold the purse strings or are key influencers. Never settle for second best. Remember 'brand you'!

So how do you make your presentation to optimum effect? What are the particular challenges you will face when presenting in English? Is there any way you can actually use this to your benefit? You might find it helpful to approach these questions from different angles. You could ask yourself:

■ Do I want to remind readers in a positive (not apologetic) way that I am not a native English writer?

■ Can I actively get them on my side by asking them to stop me at any time to explain anything that I may not have made entirely clear?

■ Do I want to impress them with perfectly composed slides written in perfect English?

You need to have confidence in your ability from the start. It is quite common, and self-defeating, for presenters in their own language and to an audience of their own nationality to apologize before they have uttered one word. Like me, you will have heard this type of thing on numerous occasions:

'I'm sorry if this seems unprepared: I didn't have much advance notice.'

'Please forgive me in advance; I'm quite nervous about presenting.'

These are unnecessary signs of weakness. They are like saying: 'This is not going to be good. I know it and you'll know it soon enough.' You get your audience wondering why they bothered to come. So instead create a position of strength. Face your audience confidently and invite them to stop you at any stage if they need you to explain the words you use. By doing this:

- they sense your confidence;

- they sense that you know what you are talking about – and what your slides are written about;

- they appreciate your care in helping them follow where you lead.

Avoiding distractions

One way of keeping people from getting distracted is to talk them through a roadmap. Manage expectations. This roadmap must also be written down and plain for all to see – be it on a flipchart as part of your introduction or even on a handout. This is why you need great English business writing skills.

Create and explain a structure to your presentation and stick to it. It means that people can navigate that written path with you and will not get lost, even if momentarily diverted for any reason (for example, if a latecomer interrupts).

What distracts you?

Probably your main distraction during any presentation is any questioning. While questions are an important form of interaction (which I will shortly deal with) there are cases where questions will answer themselves during the course of a well-prepared presentation. To avoid having to answer questions that you know are subsequently covered, you can save time by asking attendees to write their questions down.

Then ask them to save these questions for the end of the presentation. Many will then tell you that they were covered, as you anticipated.

Once again we can see how useful writing can be. It may be silent but it is an immensely important factor in successful presentations in English within global companies. People who do not work internationally often fail to grasp the importance of this. Which means that you can easily be one step ahead of your competitors!

What do readers say distracts them?

A lot of people admit that they do get distracted when:

- a slide contains a word they do not understand;
- there is a spelling or grammatical mistake;
- there is a flaw in logic.

People may not mean to focus on these but they often do. It can have the unfortunate effect that they lose focus on subsequent points as a result. Although some people may query a point, the majority tend not to interrupt a presentation to ask for an explanation. This may be polite – but they can miss the point and you can lose the business.

I knew you would ask that!

Every time you prepare your presentation, keep in mind that it should be leading to a dialogue. For instance, for every 15 minutes of presenting there could be 5 minutes of follow-up discussion. There may then be the questions that your presentation has not been able to cover. So try to ensure that any questioning takes you forwards towards your goals, not backwards away from them. If your presentation is not clear or if there are mistakes on your slides, people will ask the wrong questions. It can take their and your focus away from the primary objectives of your pitch.

So your presentation in English actually starts at the writing stage. This is when you ask yourself: what could be asked here? Write bullet points to outline the issue. Presenters who fail to do this are the ones who are heard exclaiming: 'I knew you would ask that!' when questioned by a member of their audience. An unkind questioner could reply: 'Well, if you knew I would ask that, then why didn't you cover it?'

There is a serious message here. Your audience might act as if such a situation were amusing but they could actually be offended by your omission. Their unspoken feelings might be that if you knew they would ask the question, then why are you wasting their time by not giving the answers they need?

Further tips for making life easier

Create an opportunity for follow-up dialogue in writing

If I do not already have attendees' e-mail addresses (for example, if I am giving a public talk) I ask the audience to give me their addresses if they would like a summary e-mailed to them after the event. This is useful for them, as I always include useful tips. It is useful for me too, as it takes me into a future with those people.

My half-hour talk may be over on that day but I will schedule more time with those delegates. I am not cold-calling them: they have asked for more, so it becomes an ongoing dialogue in writing. That is a great business result.

Eliminate the guesswork; rely on yourself

Most presentations today are electronic. This can easily lead to problems: unfamiliar systems, power failures etc. I guarantee you know what I mean! Another reason why a good written preparation (at least for yourself) makes sure you can carry on. Do not rely purely on technology; rely on yourself.

If there are any words or English acronyms of a technical nature on your slides, take the time to ensure that your audience has really understood what you mean. This is particularly important in multi-cultural groups. People are often reluctant to speak up for fear of embarrassment, but it is also more common than you may think that people convince themselves of an entirely incorrect meaning of a word based on something similar from their own language. Do not be afraid to ask and clarify – you all benefit in the end. Eliminate the guesswork.

Visuals

Great visuals can reinforce your writing. In fact, a good picture can 'speak volumes'. But do ensure that your pictures fit that writing. Once again, it is likely to be a question of mixing and matching to suit your target audience at the time. Be aware, for example, that some people love tables and pie charts. Others hate them.

Even colours can be lucky or unlucky, depending on cultural sensibility. So if you are pitching to a particular country, choosing colours from their flag may be a very useful way of knowing which colours will work.

Your checklist for action

■ Prepare well and plan your words with confidence.

■ Make the right impact – remember 'brand you'.

■ Realize that presentations can be a new format for business reports: the words on your slides and handouts are 'business writing' that can be forwarded to others and read after the speech has been forgotten.

■ Therefore ensure that your slides are in well-written English.

■ Explain any technical terms, English acronyms etc that may be in your slides.

■ Give your audience a clear written roadmap through your presentation.

■ Do not let written English errors on your slides cause distractions.

■ Anticipate likely questions and try to write answers in your presentation.

■ Consider what will work and what might not for your particular audience: visuals, colours etc.

■ Try to create a dialogue in your slides and handouts that will continue after your talk.

5

We all need to write to market and sell

Everyone is an ambassador and salesperson

In Chapter 2, I highlighted how it helps us achieve our business English writing objectives by embracing the fact that we can all actively market our organization and sell its messages every time we write. We fail when our audience finds our writing ineffective. Feedback suggests that this can result from it coming across as:

- over-complicated;
- uncaring;
- written by a 'jobsworth' type of person;

- sloppily presented, with mistakes;

- full of jargon;

- impersonal.

Ineffective writing will imply that you have put the shutters up and closed the door. Given a choice, your customers may well walk away. Unless to make a complaint, they will not necessarily call again. The good news is that your audience is likely to give your writing their full approval when they are able to see and say:

- It is in my or our interests.

- I know what I must do, why, how and when.

- I or we feel appreciated.

- This is definitely the product or service or message etc of choice.

You simply have to achieve this approval to be an effective ambassador and salesperson for your organization, whatever your actual job specification.

Writing is a key that opens the door

In the past, a customer's first contact with an organization was often more likely to be by telephone than by writing. If you were promoting a message or actively selling in your job, this could offer you an advantage. When you hear a voice, you have an opportunity (however fleeting) to ask questions and, even better, try to develop rapport.

Increasingly these days, the first point of contact with a prospective client is when they write an e-mail. It is cheap, easy and fast for them to do this – and they can keep their distance from you. So if you are really going to be proactive in your job (and I hope you are), you may have to work that little bit harder, to make your English business writing the key that opens the door to new or continuing business.

Writing must be an effective point of contact

How can you achieve this? Try analysing other people's writing to get some answers. Why not start by looking at things as if you are the consumer about to make a purchase? Imagine you sent a request for information and you have two pitches from two different companies. Imagine that the services provided and their prices are the same – but one company sends a professional, courteous e-mail, the other a poorly presented one.

Which one are you likely to favour? Feedback consistently suggests that most people will be drawn to the former. It is a common perception that an organization that cares about presentation is likely to have a professional, quality, systematic approach generally. Writing well is an opportunity to open that door to new customers. Never waste it.

Just a few months ago, a jobseeker sent me an unsolicited letter and CV, and asked for a job with my consultancy. She wrote that she was a communication skills training professional. Fair enough; the English she used was good. But overall she was not professional enough, because her letter – that crucial first point of contact – was covered with coffee stains. Why did she not realize that a prospective employer would probably make an initial judgement based on that? Could I let someone present such a sloppy image to my clients? And what did it say about her attitude to me personally? Did I not deserve a clean sheet of paper (and the respect that this implies), especially as she perceived me as a potential boss?

These factors all come into the business writing equation. And my view is shared by others. In fact, time after time, recruitment managers tell me they throw badly written letters and e-mailed applications from jobseekers directly into the waste bin. Procurement managers do the same with shoddily presented bids and proposals. This can apply even where huge international contracts are involved.

Mostly it is to do with the standard of written English, because if you cannot be bothered to match the brief, or even get your potential clients' details right, why should you get the contract? What does it say about you compared with the people who take the care to get it right?

Try to look at your own writing objectively, as your readers will. That way, you will soon manage to identify the words, formats and also the presentation of material that make the right impact. Your writing will build bridges to enable readers to cross to your side instead of pushing them away as a lot of writing does, totally unintentionally, especially in cross-cultural scenarios.

Advertising and promotional literature for a global market

Companies can fail to realize that points that may be of interest to a local market may be of little relevance to a global audience. Thus we may have a company proudly announcing in the opening lines of their new brochure:

Jones Management Services Ltd

Based in the south of England, Jones Management Services Ltd have been established for 60 years and have amalgamated with four other local companies in that time, closing down satellite offices in order to consolidate in one city-centre site.

The company are highly accredited management services providers to clients from diverse areas. It is their insistence on maintaining first-class credentials that makes Jones stand apart from other providers in helping companies succeed internationally.

This company has wasted the first three lines – which should always be dedicated to engaging an audience's attention. Prospective clients probably do not need a complete history of a provider's previous local office accommodation, even if they are only targeting that local market. Surely Jones's key message for an international audience is:

Building on a solid history of 60 years' success and first-class credentials, Jones Management Services have unrivalled expertise in helping companies succeed internationally.

In short, open your horizons as you write. Do not just translate the brochure and the details you may include in your own language. Trading internationally may require a totally different mindset, coupled with a different advertising angle – and probably different words.

Sales letters must enable that call to action

It is remarkable how often writers forget that they should be promoting their message each time they write. Even professional salespeople can miss obvious opportunities that writing presents to enable calls to action: that is, to help prospective buyers actually buy.

If, for example, you are trying to sell insurance in English and you send details of your company policy to someone who has made an enquiry, why end your pitch as so many sales people do, with flat, lacklustre words? Contrast these two examples:

'Please do not hesitate to call for further information.'

'I will call about this next Tuesday, if this is convenient.'

Be proactive and enable that call to action in whichever way is right for your customer. Then do what you have said in writing you will do. If you have said you will phone, then make sure you do. This crucially important tip applies to everything you send out, not just sales letters. Your writing is judged for what it is.

International readers are particularly likely to focus on the literal meaning of every word you write. What does it say about you and your organization if you promise something that you have no intention of delivering? This is not good news, is it? Would you buy from someone like that?

Beyond the very obvious courtesy to your reader of doing as you say you will, another factor comes into play. If you tell someone you will be making contact, you improve the chance that they will keep your letter in their in-tray. There are no guarantees, but if they are even half interested in your proposal, they will be expecting your call. It makes it less of a cold call, which acts in your favour.

I once received a mailshot from a Mercedes-Benz dealer. It impressed me, in principle, as it explained the company's aim to offer 'a more personal approach to the business user'. The writer had included her photo in the letter and she looked professional and personable. Whatever the size of company – from the one-person operator through to the fleet manager of the largest company – she was on hand, to offer guidance and advice. She ended the mailshot:

> 'I will give you a call in the next few days to see what arrange-
> ments we can make.'

So she had built up an expectation on the reader's part. As it happened, I was quite interested ('a hot lead' in sales talk) and was a prospective client. I was keen to know what she would say when she called. And do you know what happened? Nothing; the call never came. This led me to think: why did she write that?

If the timescale was unrealistic – say, because she could not make all the calls she had promised to make in the 'next few days' – then why had she set that deadline? Setting a timescale was her decision, after all. Not to deliver on her promise undermined her performance and that of her company, in my (and no doubt other readers') estimation.

Setting deadlines in writing

Let's develop this point. If we feel that setting a deadline is going to help us, then let's make sure that the deadline is one that we can meet. And it makes sense for our international target audience: time-zone considerations can come into play. Tuesday is not always Tuesday, depending on where you are in the world.

You can even impress readers by setting a deadline that you know you can beat. So, for example, if you write, 'I will deliver this information by Friday 12th March,' and you actually deliver it on Wednesday 10th March, two days before, then your recipient may be delighted.

Are you planning to buy?

Here are some standard English expressions that you may be able to use or adapt:

Thank you for your recent quotation and please find our order attached.

With reference to our telephone conversation earlier today, please can you confirm receipt of the enclosed order by letter or e-mail?

Please could you deal with this as a matter of urgency?

Can you offer a volume discount? (a discount for large orders)

We reserve the right to refuse faulty stock / to refuse goods delivered after the agreed date.

Please confirm that we will receive the delivery by mid December.

Your competitors offer significantly lower prices; can you match them?

Can you deliver anywhere worldwide?

Are you selling?

Here are more English examples that you may find helpful:

Thank you for your provisional order. We enclose our invoice for €800. On receipt of your payment, we will be pleased to despatch your order within seven days.

We are pleased to confirm your order. All items are in stock and we will advise you of the delivery date shortly.

We regret that items 1 and 2 are currently out of stock. Would you like us to order these for you?

Your order was sent by airfreight yesterday and should be with you within a few days.

The shipment is due to arrive on 6 July.

All orders placed during the exhibition are subject to a 10% discount.

Our prices are subject to currency fluctuations.

We would like to offer a free, no-obligation consultation.

Do not mislead your buyers or be misled by sellers

There are some regrettable instances where you may get your English advertising totally correct yet still alienate your customers. An example that springs to mind is this. A student advertised a new Xbox 360 box online. He described it as the hit of the year; it was brand new and he had the product receipt. He also included some small print: 'You are bidding on an authentic Xbox 360 box.'

Demand was high, bidding went up and up and he sold at a much higher price than the recommended retail price of the Xbox product at the time. The trouble was, the buyer found to his cost that he had bought a new, empty box. His expectation was that he was buying the box plus product that he assumed was inside. When he looked again at the advertisement, the empty box he actually received did fit the description. It really was only the box that was being advertised. There was no illegal claim – and therefore no fraud – involved. As a result, the buyer had no way of seeking his money back or gaining any other form of compensation.

I have three tips here:

■ Make sure that your writing does not mislead, either intentionally or unintentionally. We should care far too much about our readers and our customers ever to run the risk of deceiving or otherwise alienating them.

■ Make sure that you always read (and if necessary re-read) writing carefully, so that you understand what the print (especially small print) is telling you.

■ If you are not sure on any level, check before you proceed to the next stage!

Chasing payment: one style does not suit all

If you ever send letters or e-mails chasing people for non-payment of accounts, you will know that customers fall into different groups. So should you really send the same wording to really valued customers as you send to those who are or may be a bad risk? Naturally all customers matter – but when it comes to payment, you need to receive it to survive. So let me give you some tips to help you.

Writing to a valued customer

There will never be one formula that we can use for our business writing, as we should always customize our writing for our organization's and our audience's needs. That said, the following extract softens the tone so that customers know they need to settle their account, without the request being too abrasive.

> We do not appear to have received payment for invoice RD78 for £780.57, which was due at the end of last month, in accordance with the agreed terms.
>
> Please could you make payment within seven days, or let us know if there are any problems of which we are unaware.
>
> If you have already paid this account, please ignore this letter and accept our apologies.

Writing to a customer who you feel is a bad risk

The following is an extract from a letter a company is sending out to a customer who has ignored requests to pay an account:

> You have not replied to our letters of 18 January or 22 February and we have been instructed by our accounts department to request immediate payment of this overdue account.
>
> Payment should be made to this office at the above address within the next seven days, or we may have no alternative but to take further action to recover this amount.

You can see how the style is much heavier handed than the first example. This style should only be used when there is a real problem – and it is very regrettable when companies use it too readily. Customers are precious and we offend them at our peril.

Once you have identified that a final demand – rather than a request for payment – is appropriate, then you need to make it clear that the customer must pay. Nevertheless, you can see how the passive construction 'we have been instructed by our accounts department' helps the writer make the situation less personal? This conveys the sense that any (implied) legal action against the customer will be initiated by a department, not by the writer. This extract shows that in certain situations the English passive form can be useful.

Where the writer moves back to the active construction 'or we may have no alternative but to take further action,' they still manage to soften the harshness of approach slightly by using the verb 'may' rather than 'will'.

Your checklist for action

■ Writing English for international business is a key that opens the door to business – and that can keep it open.

■ Avoid upsetting customers or potential customers through unclear or inappropriate business English writing.

■ Try to encourage follow-on action or dialogue in writing.

■ Be aware that writing can be a permanent record: be sure you can deliver what you propose. Never mislead.

6

Making an impact through written word power

The wow factor sets you apart

Great writing is how you can make your mark and it sets you apart from the rest. Why not be proud to make a difference and improve performance too? After all, nobody ever made it to the top by blending in. The right impact puts you in pole position to secure the right responses and sell whatever it is you need to sell. The wow factor can be as simple as words that stand out from the page.

Powerful descriptions sell

For practical examples let's look at the world of online auctions. Two separate sellers each has one of two identical brand new CDs to sell. Seller 1 simply lists the CD's title (and spells it wrong) and names the asking price. Seller 2 writes the CD's title correctly and also mentions the fact it is brand new and one of the most acclaimed CDs of the year. He sets out fully correct information in a most professional manner, and asks a considerably higher price than Seller 1.

You may think the better price will win each time – but this is not always the case. On occasion the one with the power wording will sell for double the price. The more expensive the product, the greater this effect is, because people will often pay a premium for the right quality.

Let's stay with online auction sites. It may surprise you that even when it comes to buying large specialist items, a written description may be the most important aspect that a potential buyer has to focus on. As an illustration, imagine you are selling a power generator online. You have a potential buyer who is not going to be able to try it out and is very unlikely to find a product test or review. He has narrowed it down to two models: yours and a competitor's. The two models are very similar: indeed, a buyer may even suspect they were made at the same factory under different brand names. Yet the price difference between the two could be as much as 300 per cent. Seller 1 has posted a picture and price. Seller 2 has added a description using written English power words such as 'state of the art', 'reliable' and 'guaranteed'.

Once again, a dynamic, comprehensive written description makes the words stand out. This in turn makes the product stand out and all of this engages buyers' attention. Ultimately, it sells.

Good written words can create a following

Good written words not only make people pay attention and buy the goods or services you are offering, they can create a following too. This means that people will be more likely to buy from you in the future. They may ask you to develop your range if they like what you have already provided.

So if you are failing to see the potential that well-chosen English writing has to open doors, improve performance and actually boost profits, then you are certainly failing to use word power. Why do that, when the power to choose the best words for your business is an undoubtedly crucial step on any ladder to success?

Word power skills

Marketing teams know that they need to identify the words that are most likely to engage their target audience's attention. After all, engagement and involvement are the first step in selling. You have to present your message in a way that your target market can and will relate to. You have to write with impact.

One thing is absolutely sure: if you are not enthusiastic about what you are selling, you lessen your chances of engaging that interest. Knowing how to harness word power is an excellent way of fusing these two strands of enthusiasm and interest in your writing. Knowing how to develop word power skills is fundamental to successful business writing. That is why I named my website www.wordpowerskills.com right from the start.

So how do you harness word power in written English? A very good start is to identify words that make the most positive impact on you. Sometimes we like the words that other people use, without realizing that maybe we too can use these words (or similar ones) to take our businesses forward. We can all make a difference. It is not just creative design agencies who have the monopoly to innovate and succeed.

Let me highlight two letter headlines and you will get a feel for what I mean. The background is the same in each case: two separate tour operators were confirming a holiday booking I had made with each. The letter from tour operator 1 had the headline 'IT'S ALL BOOKED!' The letter from tour operator 2 had the headline 'Confirmation of booking'.

Compare the two and you can sense the far greater enthusiasm in the first than in the second. The first operator has harnessed written word power. Naturally, we have to judge what is right for our target readers. For me, it certainly worked. Although e-mail etiquette suggests that it is wrong to write in upper case (because it is taken to be SHOUTING), I think it is acceptable in this letter. I do not mind if they are shouting with happiness because my holiday is arranged; I am happy too.

It is true that the second operator's headline is fit for purpose. The headline cannot be criticized for this, and it may be entirely right for the reader. But if we are always cautious writers who keep our enthusiasm hidden, we may ultimately lose out to competitors who seem pleased when things go right for their customers.

What is likely to happen once we see writing expressing that a company is delighted to have the opportunity to help with our travel arrangements? And wishes us a great holiday and thanks us for our custom? Generally, as long as we sense it is sincere, we rather like it. The company that simply confirms the booking may start to look slightly less attractive. In our estimation, we may downgrade their good performance to 'satisfactory' and may upgrade the enthusiastic company's good performance to 'excellent'. That is what harnessing word power can do.

In order to understand how to harness written word power, I suggest you look afresh at the written English words that businesses use successfully. You can do this by actively identifying words that engage your attention in a positive way. They may be words used within your own workplace, but they do not have to be. They can be words that attract us as consumers.

In the business writing workshops that I run, these are the power words that people routinely say attract them most:

free, advice without cost, value for money, low cost, cost effective;

success, successful;

now, immediate, fast, today;

easy, efficient, effective;

benefits, advantages, results;

help, support;

expert, expertise, professional, professionalism, know-how;

latest, world first;

best, excellence, first class;

safe, green, eco-friendly, energy efficient;

valued, valuable;

please, thank you.

As these are the words that consumers themselves identify as attracting their attention and buy-in, these must indeed be very powerful words. They therefore provide an excellent base for the sort of words you could and should be choosing routinely to get yourself and your organization noticed for the right reasons.

Take a moment to identify which of these words you could justifiably and comfortably use in your daily business writing. Now for a crucially important question: do you use any of them currently? If not, why not?

Remember that any list does not have to end here. Can you think of other words that you could add, to make your own customized list of business power words? My clients over the years take delight in compiling their own lists of power words. Ask your colleagues to join you in this exercise and make a list of any relevant power words, as and when they occur to you.

Power words that I (or we) should be using

Look at the world around you

Looking at the world around you is not just useful from the point of view of identifying power words. It also helps you see that making the best connections with readers can also be about designing writing where the focus is not just on you or your organization.

For example, we may buy products because they are endorsed by celebrities whose buying power gives them access to the best choices available and we may therefore think that if they use these products, then we should too. In fact, one very well-known international cosmetics retailer uses English to suggest that we buy their celebrity-endorsed products because, by implication, we are 'worth it'. They very neatly convert the self-preoccupied 'I' of the celebrity to the inclusive 'you' of the worldwide audience. The message neatly embraces all potential users.

Look at this next example of how business writing can create this engagement. I received a letter urging me to buy an insurer's 'exciting new product', namely their latest professional indemnity insurance. In my view, although they had used a power word – 'exciting' – it failed to ignite my enthusiasm. Quite simply, it was inappropriate: the product was not, indeed could never be, exciting! It came as no surprise to me therefore that the product was later relaunched with copy on the following lines:

> 'Does it concern you that there are many things you can be sued for in business? Worry no longer: our comprehensive new policy is designed to provide you with peace of mind.'

This time the message made much more sense. Even though it was not a message I liked (who wants to be sued?), it certainly highlighted why people need insurance. The negative word power in making readers feel nervous and uneasy was justified as long as the company was providing them a solution. In contrast, suggesting that the product was 'exciting' – even though this might have seemed like positive word power – was never going to make sound commercial sense. In short, if it did not result in the new business it sought, it was a waste of written word power.

Let me tell you of another instance where a company had to rewrite their advertising because they too had focused more on themselves than on their audience. A city-centre restaurant closed for a major refurbishment. The owner had leaflets printed, outlining his inspired new menu, which he planned to issue both within the restaurant and externally, after the grand reopening. The leaflets were high-quality, double-sided, glossy cards. They looked really good and the food shown appeared to cater for all tastes.

The owner paid people to hand the leaflets out at various points throughout the city. I was handed one and put it in my bag. When I got home, I liked what I saw and decided to check out where the restaurant was. And can you guess what I am going to say? There was no address, there were no contact details, there was only the restaurant's name. As the name was brand new, it was not even listed in the telephone book, nor was there a website at that time. As the leaflet had been handed out at a location that was nowhere near the restaurant, the trail was cold. What a waste of effort this involved, as well as a waste of the owner's money and readers' time, and potential loss of custom.

Some months later I saw a new leaflet being distributed for the same restaurant. It was far less impressive in terms of quality: it was now very flimsy, with very few pictures of appetizing food to grab readers' interest. The previous advertising had clearly used up much of the owner's budget. But can you guess what now appeared? A map showing how to get to the restaurant, the restaurant's full address and telephone number and e-mail address. In short, this is the writing that makes the ultimate connections with readers. It may not seem exciting, but this is the writing that enables the ultimate call to action: literally bringing customers to you.

When it comes to designing your business English writing, do not simply focus on translating from your language into English and losing sight of the key commercial considerations.

You will find many of the answers you need simply by looking at the world expressed in English around you. You will soon find it easy to analyse what works and why it works. Then all you have to do is use the elements that will work for you and your audience.

Without common sense, you will fail

Keep to the common-sense solutions!

You can have the best product or service in the world yet still fail, if you do not use common sense or make complete sense every time you write. Surprisingly, though, you never find a 'Director of Common Sense', do you?

This means there will have been quite a lot of nonsense in some business literature you will have read. Websites, brochures, presentations ... these can all be littered with claims that are utterly false, though that was never the writer's intention. One swimwear manufacturer, for example, claimed that their swimwear 'dries fast in water'. How can that be possible? Or a major retailer's claim that 'you will never find quality at a better price'. What does this mean? It is grammatically correct English – but does it make sense?

Even when you are selling a message and not a product, the storyline has to make sense. A recent charity campaign attracted unexpected complaints when it tried to show how adversity through drugs and associated violence can be overcome, but focused rather too much on the violence. The charity had to reply to these complaints by outlining the full intent of their storyline and the fact that they can help people out of this, which had been quite hidden. In short, the charity had thought that 'implying' their help was as effective as expressing it. It usually is not.

Do you know the tale of the Emperor's new clothes? If so, you will know that it took one little boy to stand up and say that the Emperor's new clothes were not the finest in the world; in fact, he actually had no clothes at all. My point is that writing with impact in business is not about making false claims in order to impress readers – because you simply will not. It is also not about assuming that your line of thought is completely clear to others.

If readers find a flaw in your logic, the follow-on effects can be manifold:

- You lose professional credibility in their eyes.
- Why should they buy in to what you are saying?
- Why should they buy in to anything else you may say in the future?
- They may walk away.
- They may complain.
- They may tell others – and this further harms your reputation.
- They will probably buy in to your competitors' messages that do make sense.

Regularly refresh your word power

It is important that organizations regularly refresh their writing, so that they are not stuck in the rut of yesteryear. In commerce, words that were right for yesterday may not be right for today; words that are right for today may not be right for tomorrow.

To illustrate, I recently saw a lorry drive past, with the words 'Quality Bulk Haulage' emblazoned on its side. I did not catch sight of the company's name, only these three words. Instead of being impressed, as one might expect, I actually thought what a meaningless expression this is. Does the word 'quality' describe bulk? In which case, what is quality bulk? I have no idea. Or is it meant to communicate 'quality haulage of bulk'? In that case, what does this involve over and above a 'lesser' bulk haulage company? Is this one faster? Is it more efficient?

I want the slogan writer to do the work for me. This is not just about choosing correct English words: it is also about spelling out a really good reason why this company is better than the rest. Or it is about grabbing my interest, so that I remember the brand if I want to find out more.

Of course, quality is both a tangible and an intangible standard that we all seek as consumers. But for advertisers to use the word validly these days, it can be better to set it within a meaningful context. Otherwise, powerful as it might be within its right context, when used in isolation it can actually be a cliché: an expression that has been overused to the point of losing its effectiveness.

Another formerly powerful English word that can become devalued through overuse is 'prestigious'. It has almost got to the point where every award ever given out is now 'prestigious'. In the same way, 'diva', formerly used (in the positive sense) to describe female singers of global renown, is increasingly used to describe female singers with just one best-selling album or even just one single. The moment you sense that your existing power words are becoming clichés is the time to identify new ones.

An introduction to customer focus in writing

Word power can really help you focus on your customers and your audience at any given time. Sometimes you can identify how to express customer focus simply by discarding elements that will not express it. These negative elements can be:

- being prepared to let readers see spelling and grammatical errors in English as our company norm;

■   writing the wrong words in the wrong place, at the wrong time;

■   conveying the wrong sentiments, such as 'don't' and 'can't' and 'won't'.

Doing these things routinely contributes to a 'don't care' scenario. Once again, in order to write effectively, simply focus on the fact that you too are a consumer. In this role, companies are competing for your attention every day. Whether it is through customized mail, impersonal junk mail, advertisements in newspapers or magazines, companies are relying on readers to become consumers. As a consumer, you will know how some business writing works really well, some works fairly well and so on, right down the scale to writing that fails to get results. Surprisingly perhaps, that is not the bottom of the pile. The worst of all is business writing that annoys and alienates those it should be attracting and supporting.

Something strange can happen when people start to write English in business. They tend to write waffle, gobbledegook, jargon, text-speak – and can completely shun the friendly yet professional writing that focuses on the fact that 'customer is king'. That is the kind of writing our readers can expect and really want from us.

Yet what can happen when our fingers touch the keyboard? How often do we use a key stroke 'as a handshake' or other method of rapport and bridge building – so necessary for our cross-cultural audiences? Or for writing that develops effective working relationships? The answer is: rarely.

So be a style detective and spot for yourself the difference in these two e-mails:

'Petra, I need the information tomorrow. Robert.
Dear Petra
We need this information tomorrow so that we succeed in our targets. Many thanks for your help in this.
Kind regards,
Robert.

Spot the clues and avoid the techniques that fail. Adopt the techniques that win, which are usually those that speak to readers at the right level. Would you agree?

Standard endings can destroy the personal touch

If you agree that the personal touch is likely to be a good thing, then avoid 'autopilot mode'. This is when companies use standard endings in English without thought.

For example, a company that manufactures carbon monoxide detectors issued a product safety recall notice, as there was a defect in a product range. The presence of poisonous concentrations of carbon monoxide was not activating the alarm in certain units, which was the entire point of their existence. So the company notified retailers and asked consumers both to remove the unit from service immediately and to return it for a full refund. The manufacturer apologized for any inconvenience caused, stating that, as customers would appreciate, safety was the primary objective of the recall. So far so good, we could say, in view of the circumstances. The risk had been assessed and was being managed effectively. However, the manufacturer then concluded with this rather standard ending to their recall:

'We would like to assure you that (our brand) is subject to the strictest safety and quality tests together with an ongoing commitment to the best in customer service levels.'

I think this wording is incomplete. There was a problem: so the company's safety and quality tests were transparently not met in this instance. They have to concede this, surely. Although the company apologized for the inconvenience caused, they did not express regret for the obvious slip-up in safety and quality standards. Simply by issuing a standard sentence that implies all is well in this respect is, strictly speaking, untrue. A carbon monoxide alarm that does not work is very bad news for the consumers who have put their trust in it. If this was a one-off occurrence in the company's history, then the company is perfectly entitled to state this – and readers may actually appreciate their openness and honesty.

What readers do not like is to feel that a company does not care about them or any adverse circumstances (major or minor) they may encounter when dealing with that company. Organizations need to realize this if they profess to care about customers and serve them well, they need to express this truthfully and with integrity, in all aspects of their business writing.

Your checklist for action

■ Set yourself and your organization apart with powerful, customer-centred writing at all times.

■ Create enthusiasm by using the right English power words and phrases.

■ Harness the wow factor in your writing as this not only sells but can also create a following.

■ Regularly refresh the power words you use, to avoid becoming clichéd.

■ Continuously learn from others' mistakes in all aspects of your business English writing.

■ Express messages clearly; simply implying facts can often fail.

■ Read your 'standard English endings' carefully before sending: they may not be appropriate in all cases.

■ Write English that will build relationships in cross-cultural business.

7

Four steps to success

The Word Power Skills system

This guide will help you communicate effectively on a daily basis by encapsulating all the messages in this book. It goes like this:

Step 1

Be correct:

- Know what your writing needs to achieve, alongside what your company needs to achieve.
- Match reader and customer expectations.
- Ensure that your writing is free of mistakes.

Your business communication will fail if you get your basics wrong.

Step 2

Be clear:

- Use plain English and express facts as simply as possible.
- Edit so that your main points are easily understood.

Confused messages undermine your objectives. They can lose you custom too.

Step 3

Make the right impact:

- Use the right words and layout to get noticed for the right reasons.
- Use the right style to present yourself and your company well.
- Write to create opportunities.

The right impact differentiates you from competitors and helps bring about the replies you need.

Step 4

Focus on your customers:

- Write from their perspective; empathize with them.
- Use positive, proactive words where possible.

■ Avoid words that put up barriers, and avoid jargon wherever you can.

Use these words to satisfy and, if possible, delight your customers.

Being correct for purpose

Step 1 in the system is about identifying why you write in business. There should always be a purpose that fits in with your personal aims, alongside your organization's values and objectives. Let's compare two opening lines in letters to see this in practice.

> 'With reference to the meeting held last week, it is hoped that the contract will be sent in any event no later than seven days from now, in an endeavour to accommodate your requirements.'

> 'It was good meeting you this week and your input was most valuable. In view of your pressing deadlines, I am ensuring that the contract will reach you no later than seven days from now.'

In the second example, the writer is creating an opportunity to express to the recipient the fact that they are valued. Beyond this, the writer is taking an initiative: to deliver to the recipient's satisfaction. Note the contrast between the tentative, impersonal approach in the first example, against the more dynamic approach in the second. We do not have the benefit of knowing the outcomes here, but written word power definitely provides an initial indicator of the likelihood of personalized, proactive, quality performance. And here is the best news of all: it has cost nothing.

Being correct also means that you check that your business writing is free of mistakes before you issue it. This is as crucial for native English writers as for non-native English writers. Why? Because readers so often make a value judgement: that mistakes equal lack of professionalism and may reflect poor products or service. As an illustration, compare the opening lines from two covering letters sent with a CV:

'as You reguest I atach My cv and the application from in respekt of the post advertised.'

'As you request, I attach my CV and application form in respect of the post advertised.'

The second example is correctly written; the first contains a number of mistakes. Unfortunately for the writer, the chances are high that the recruiter will dismiss this application and immediately throw it away. Although this may seem harsh, it happens again and again. Recruiters consistently report that for every mistake-riddled application there are likely to be others that are right. They are written by applicants who have taken the time to check their forms, check their English – and who are prepared to ask someone to help if necessary. Companies appreciate these applicants' understanding of how important it is to get writing right. It can make all the difference to whether an applicant gets to interview stage, which, after all, is that essential first foot in the door.

Write clearly

You write clearly when you highlight key messages concisely. Writing informative headings, subheadings and short sentences can have the very real advantage of not overloading our readers. There is the added benefit that this aligns with the move towards plain English and simple sentences in business writing today. The demand is largely driven by customers and top management, so we ignore this development at our peril.

But be aware that too many short sentences can create an ineffective style. The key to writing success is to design interesting text and layout, including varied sentence length. As a general rule, most business writers try to keep a sentence to a maximum of 25 words. Some even say 20 words, though to be so prescriptive is not an absolute must. If you do have a lot of information to write, try devices such as:

- bullet lists or numbered points to break up an otherwise large chunk of text;

- emboldened subheadings that work as additional points of interest, and grab attention in their own right;

- an appendix (or appendices) or Word® document attachments. But do make sure that these are in English. In multi-cultural environments these attachments are often in a different language, which the target audience will not understand.

How simplicity can free you to impress

If people are able to understand quickly what you write, you benefit from being able to focus on what really matters: getting your key messages across. This applies whether you have a public announcement to make or need to outline why you are the supplier of choice.

If you are writing in English as a non-native English writer you may find that your natural instinct is to focus on the translation from your own language into English. That is when you may become preoccupied with the translation. You can find yourself unintentionally focusing only on a description of features rather than on a crucially important outline of the benefits. This is what my non-NE clients tell me time after time.

In essence, you may find yourself falling into the trap of out-Englishing or over-Englishing the English, the syndrome I mentioned previously. This is the self-imposed trap of choosing the most complicated vocabulary out of any list you see, particularly when using online dictionaries. I cannot stress enough that readers generally do not want this: they yearn for simply expressed facts. These get messages across faster and reduce the chance of misunderstandings. It follows that simple writing is therefore also going to cost less than complicated writing.

To help you get into the habit of choosing the simplest words in English each time, just take a look at the following list of words or phrases. In each case, I list a complex word followed by a simpler word with the same meaning.

assist ... help

visualize ... see

purchase ... buy

state ... say

sufficient ... enough

approximately ... about

require ... need

in order that ... so that

statutory ... legal

due to the fact that ... because

ascertain ... check

materialize ... happen

supplementary cost ... extra cost

Plain English

Writing plain English is about choosing simple English words over complex ones, as I have just demonstrated. It is about using accessible English words that will make more impact in global business – precisely because people are more likely to understand what they mean.

Increasingly, one aspect of plain English is about converting passive mood into active mood. Broadly speaking, the difference between the two modes is as follows:

The active voice is where the subject does the action; for example: 'Nao Eno gave the keynote talk about exporting to new markets.'

The passive voice is where the subject of the active clause becomes secondary. The subject may appear acted upon, or receives the action. Often the word 'by' is added, as follows: 'The keynote talk on exporting to new markets was given by Nao Eno.'

In both examples, it is clear that Nao Eno gave the talk – but the first is clearer (especially for non-NE readers) and has the advantage of using fewer words. There are times when using the passive leads to a loss of ownership of the matter reported. For example: 'A keynote talk on exporting to new markets was given to the conference.' Readers are no longer informed that Nao Eno gave the talk. If people were unimpressed by his performance, he might be pleased about this. But if his speech received rapturous applause, he might be very upset that his name did not appear.

Using the passive too readily, without evaluating whether it is the right mode, can also make writing appear old-fashioned and even pompous. It is often unclear as to who does what. In fact, passives can make it seem unnecessary for anyone to do anything. For example: 'Consideration should be given as to whether this amount should be calculated as part of the amount outstanding or be passed over to the finance department to be reconciled.'

There is a lack of ownership and direction right at the beginning of the sentence. By using the phrase 'consideration should be given', the writer highlights that something probably should be done, out of two possibilities (calculating an amount or passing the matter to the finance department to be reconciled). But they do not explain what actually must be done – or who will take ownership for overseeing this. So the meaning is not entirely clear. It is not plain English. This can have a significant effect in minute writing, which I address in Chapter 10.

However, there are times when you would be justified in using the passive in English. For example, there are occasions where it is best not to blame someone for a problem. Imagine you have to write to a valued customer about a possible oversight on their part. Notice how the passive form in the first sentence below is more customer-friendly and therefore suitable than the active form in the second sentence.

'It appears that your monthly instalment has not yet been paid.'

'You have not paid your monthly instalment.'

Gobbledegook

This word (also sometimes written as gobbledygook) signifies meaningless, unintelligible or pretentious language, often presented as bureaucratic jargon. There are many online forums that have sprung up to discuss this subject, especially as gobbledegook can make people laugh. However, this is never its writers' aim. They think that their erudite, circumlocutory style underlines their intelligence when the reverse is true. Did you see the gobbledegook I used in the last sentence? If you had to reach for the dictionary, you will see my point. Gobbledegook refers to the use of many words (often complicated ones) where a few would do, in a mistaken effort to highlight the writer's knowledge.

Gobbledegook is as much written by native English writers as by non-NE writers. Here is an example. An estate agent (or realtor in US English) wanted to write about a substantial fall in house prices, as sellers were reducing their asking prices. He wrote: 'The substantial drops in asking prices are further confirmation of the underlying trend of more sellers readjusting their prices downwards.'

His writing did make an impact but unfortunately for him and his company, for the wrong reasons. It was gobbledegook and it made the sentence rather ridiculous. The way we write does not have to be so different from the way we speak. We don't have to build in complexity: certainly not if we want to be noticed for the right reasons.

Structuring your writing

Before you even begin to write a sentence in English, it helps to identify which are the main points you wish to make and which are subsidiary. Then design your writing so that every word earns its place and adds value. The good news is that sometimes all it takes is simple tweaking of our copy to improve performance dramatically. Sometimes addressing structure means avoiding the autopilot writing mode to which I have previously referred. Here is an example. I received a covering letter attached to an invoice. This extract makes the point:

> Please find enclosed our invoice for the services provided, as agreed.
>   May we take this opportunity of thanking you for your custom?
>   **PLEASE MAKE PAYMENT WITHIN 30 DAYS PAYABLE TO SMITH INC.**

The invoice the company had attached to this covering note set out the payment terms in full, so there was no need to repeat this message in the covering note. So what was the point of the covering letter? Surely its purpose was to take the opportunity to thank the person or company for their custom? The writer had identified that this was a good idea, but what had he done then? He had eclipsed this great customer-centred message by a writer-centred message. This was emphasized in capital letters, in effect shouting 'PAY US SOON'.

Your checklist for action

■ Remember the four steps: correctness, clarity, impact and customer focus.

▓ Plan your key points before you even start writing your document in English.

▓ Structure your writing and make use of the right power words for impact, clarity and involvement.

▓ Try to use active constructions coupled with simple, plain English.

▓ Avoid over-complicated words and check that you are not writing gobbledegook.

8

Writing press releases and editorial

Create the right publicity

There is a saying in English that 'all publicity is good publicity'. I am not altogether sure about that – but good publicity is certainly worthwhile. Paying for advertising is naturally one route to promoting what you are about. Writing your own interesting copy is another – and it can be a very easy, low-cost and highly effective option. With the tips this book has already given you about how to make impact, you now have a series of different writing options. They include:

- Writing a newsworthy press release that highlights you, your staff, your cause, charity, product or service if, for example, you have received a major donation, won a major contract or award, or made some groundbreaking innovation.

■ Using your expert professional knowledge to write an article for publication.

■ Writing a contribution to a topical, professional debate featured in a newspaper or magazine.

■ Writing a free tips column on your specialism in a newspaper or magazine on a one-off or regular basis.

If you are published, the very fact that an editor has chosen you, and probably over others, gives you a great endorsement as a professional, even without any money changing hands. Readers are often sceptical about claims made in paid advertisements, which they naturally view as subjective. In contrast, they are more likely to see editorial coverage as objective. They may take more notice and react more positively as a result.

Editors are generally passionate about their publications. They will not last long in the job if they are not. As they have a vast array of unsolicited press releases coming through each week, they can choose the ones they think the best. These are likely to be:

■ those of most general interest to their readers;

■ those of most specific interest to their readers in terms of news topicality, ongoing debate etc;

■ the best written ones, that can be published as they are without the need for editing or to correct their English.

In your home country you will have an instinct for which publications to target. All you need to do then is tailor your content to your market. If you are looking for new global markets, you need to research appropriate publications and gather local knowledge, either by asking around or engaging professional public relations services. Whatever you do, make sure that you retain accountability and own the content, so ensure that the writing:

- presents your message correctly;

- is written in perfect English;

- is fit for purpose;

- is published at the right time (especially important when you are promoting something);

- contains some call to action or way to respond, to create a dialogue;

- has your name and contact details.

Different words and styles for different target publications

Even within a single country, the publications you may target can have very different styles of written English. Within the UK, at one end of the spectrum, certain British tabloids can have very informal, sensational headlines, often based on colloquial puns. Others remain far more formal. Be aware of this – and that there can be additional cultural factors to understand, before you even start writing your news item or press release.

Standard press release layout

A standard layout for a press release in English is often as follows:

- Insert the release date.

- Insert an interesting, attention-grabbing title.

- Mark the release 'For editor's attention'.

- Insert personal or organization contact details. This is so that the editor or journalist can contact a named person if they need any further information prior to publishing the release or their abridged version of it.

- If the named person is someone other than you, make sure that you have their agreement and they are aware of the release.

- Type the document in double spacing and ensure that it is immaculately presented and free of mistakes.

- The first paragraph should contain all the key information and make the point of the release clear.

- Avoid jargon and highlight the benefits to a wide audience.

- Explain the importance of the press release.

- Make it relevant to the publication, its readership or the professional field in question.

- If possible, give a short, enthusiastic and interesting quote from a named spokesperson.

- Repeat the personal or organization contact details at the end.

It is well worth remembering that editors reserve the right to edit your copy, however well you have written it. They have to use the space available to their best advantage, not yours. This is how the following scenario occurred.

A UK government agency issued a press release to promote a business event regarding trade opportunities with India. High-ranking officials would attend, to inform and help any interested businesses. It was to be a morning event, followed by networking and a free Indian lunch buffet. Any business person wishing to attend was directed towards an individual whose contact details were given.

This was how the press release was published. But can you see how two important details were omitted? They were details that would matter to anyone who might wish to attend: namely the date and the venue of the meeting. Apparently the details had appeared in the original release but the editor of the newspaper had taken them out. Presumably this was so that the release fitted the space available in that paper on that day.

Luckily, the press release did work – in the sense that any reader who might have been interested in attending the event could contact the organizer to find out more. But it did not work as well for the organizer as it should have done. Many readers might not have bothered to try to find out more. Readers expect an easy call to action; otherwise they might do nothing.

How can you ensure that editors keep in your key points? I find that marking 'For editor's attention' at the top of the release and highlighting the key points does help. Without a doubt, relationship building helps too, as you will see from this standard layout, which I have used successfully on very many occasions:

TQI press release – dd/yyyy/mm

Note to editor: for the attention of Joan Wei

As discussed in our telephone conversation, please can you ensure that the date and venue of the workshop definitely appear in the published version this week. An e-mail confirmation would be greatly appreciated.

If you need any further information please contact me on (telephone number or e-mail address).

Many thanks.

Fiona Talbot

Release for (date) issue

Better English, better business: initiative to help both regional and international businesses flourish

Do falling standards in business literacy matter to business? A surprising number of businesses believe in 'quality communication' but fail to make the connection that falling standards of English have a negative effect on their business communication.

Internationally known business writing expert Fiona Talbot, of city-centre based TQI Word Power Skills consultancy, has this to say: 'How can organizations really assure quality performance if they present mistakes in what is, after all, a vital core activity? A company needs to deliver its message clearly, consistently and well in order to succeed.'

A national Better English project has been set up to improve standards right from when pupils start learning. This is because when children are unable to read, write, speak or listen, it blocks their progress in all aspects of the curriculum, not just English. It does not stop there: the Confederation of British Industry has noted that new entrants to the workplace need help from managers with their business communication skills – which is an unwelcome burden in terms of time and resources.

TQI Word Power Skills is stepping in to help this national initiative by offering six regional businesses free consultations, business writing coaching and editing services – for one day only – on (date) from (times) at its offices at (address).

To ensure that you are one of the lucky businesses to benefit from this opportunity (which is limited to the first six companies to enrol) simply call Fiona Talbot on (telephone) or e-mail her at (e-mail address).

Ends

Words to help your press release make an impact

The way you write your headline sets the scene for your copy. Just contrast these two headlines:

Spectacular year for ABC

Very good year for ABC

The first grabs readers' attention and interest much more, through use of the dynamic word 'spectacular' and the use of bold text. This pattern is repeated in the next two examples.

Contract delight for ABC workers

Contract won by ABC

The first example introduces a further step over the second: the human element. It is a good move, given that the people factor is something that every organization's success is really built on. So use the tips given in Chapter 4: use words to make the right impact.

Evaluate every word you choose, because you have the power to choose the right words! As an example, think carefully about whether you really want to describe the award you have won as 'prestigious'. It is a great word in isolation – but if four press releases in the same publication use it, it becomes a cliché and loses impact. And is the company that announces it is second in class for the fourth year running really saying the right thing? Yes, being second is good: it means you know you can always be better. But for some readers, being second in class shouts out, 'You failed to win!' There is always going to be the right word in English, so use it.

Product recall press releases

Product recall notices are often written in very formal English. For example:

Press release by ABC regarding (name of product)

It has come to the company's notice that there may be a problem with (name of product), and a decision has been taken to recall the product, due to the possible risk to purchasers.

Anyone thus affected should return (the product), together with the appropriate receipt, to any of the company's stores nationwide in order that a full reimbursement can be made.

It has been decided to take this action as a precautionary measure in the interests of health and safety and any inconvenience caused is regretted.

Should any purchasers require any further information, a helpline is contactable at (details).

Ends

Many readers will find this writing rather old-fashioned English. They find that more informal writing conveys the message better and is more relevant today. But just how light in tone should any precautionary notification become?

Let's analyse the following product recall press release. The real-life background is this. A retailer sells axes. They find out that the head of an axe in their range can become detached from the axe handle. Naturally they need to issue a product recall fast – so let's look at the gist of their recall release.

They wrote that their axe range 'would be fantastic, were it not for the fact that the head can become detached from the handle – but thankfully, no one has been hurt'. They went on to apologize in very reader-friendly terms, even offering a full refund without a receipt. On first reading, the press release seems masterly. It is innovative; it uses the English language as people actually use it and, very importantly, it shows accountability and regret. On closer analysis, though, it might cause offence – which was certainly not intended. It has also not been fully thought through. And this is one of the supreme challenges that business writing in English (indeed any language) presents. More often than not, it has to make as much sense tomorrow, next month or even next year – not just today.

So let's think further about this piece of company writing. There is actually nothing 'fantastic' (their word) about an axe that has a design fault that could have such serious consequences. Someone could be injured, possibly very badly injured, even killed, as a direct result. Now, although the press release states that 'thankfully, no one has been hurt', when we examine this statement more closely, it does not stand up to scrutiny.

Why not? Because newspapers and other publications have deadlines for copy insertion at least a couple of days before going to press. How can you claim that 'no one has been hurt' when you know the faulty product is still available and possibly in use? What does this illogical claim say about your company? The most you can validly claim at the time you place your release is this: 'Thankfully, at the time of writing, we are unaware that anyone has been hurt.' But this becomes an awkward sentence to write – and to read. The extra words do not really add much value, if any. The sentiment may come across as jokey and if you or a relative or friend have been injured as a result of the axe's defect, you will be offended by what you will perceive as a contrived, false joke.

Let me also reinforce a message I have already given in terms of writing generally. Whenever you have to place any notice or advertisement in a publication, or indeed have any piece of writing to send out that is time specific, then do make sure that readers see it at the right time. It is absolutely useless to you if readers find out about your promotion or fundraising or whatever it is after the event is over. You defeat your own objectives and you look foolish. Once again, writing well is not just about focusing on your English; it is about focusing on every aspect that will make your message succeed.

Jargon in advertising and public relations

Jargon can be defined as words or expressions used by a particular profession or group that are difficult (often unnecessarily difficult) for others to understand. Jargon is not just used by specialists to specialists, as its users might have us believe. It can spill over to the outside world, to external readers who may be prospective customers too. This is where problems arise.

Look at this commonplace example from an advertising brochure: 'Freda Johnson, Financial Services Adviser: in partnership with Maximize UR Investment, one of the UK's leading IFAs.' If you do not know what IFA stands for, why would you be impressed? The acronym stands for Independent Financial Adviser, yet this is never explained, even though customers need to know.

In another instance where an acronym has become second nature to users but jargon to outsiders, an editor of a business magazine wrote an interesting article praising the value of RDAs. Interesting that is, if readers understood what 'RDAs' meant in this context. The editor never once explained what the acronym represented, and this made the whole article incomprehensible to many, if not most, readers.

Incidentally, here 'RDA' means Regional Development Agencies. There could have been quite a number of alternatives and it is hardly fair on readers to imply, 'Work out what I mean from the clues that the context of the article will give you.' Such a challenge, interesting though it might be, is not what the casual reader expects or wants.

Outsourcing your public relations

Many organizations find it makes financial sense to outsource their public relations and marketing material. If you decide to do this, let me give you a word of advice. You still need to manage this arrangement well because, in the final analysis, you cannot ever outsource your overall accountability for your corporate communication.

Here is an example of a scenario where outsourcing went wrong because the client company did not manage the arrangement well. A major transport provider decided to give customers the opportunity to give feedback on how the provider could improve service levels. The organization designed an outline feedback form and commissioned an external agency to conduct the customer survey campaign. The agency was given a free hand to design the final version of the feedback form, to issue the form throughout passenger arrival and departure halls, to analyse the subsequent replies and submit campaign findings back to the client.

The provider's intentions were first class. They considered that their services were good. Being customer-driven, they wanted to know how they could improve them. Unfortunately for them, an unseen problem emerged somewhere along the line, during the outsourced phase. A considerable number of typographical errors appeared in the feedback forms the agency designed and printed. Many customers returned the forms, ignoring the errors. That was the good news.

The bad news was that a surprisingly high number of customers did use their pens – but not to make positive suggestions, as the provider had hoped. Instead they highlighted each typographical error, in order to make two points of their own. First, that they were very aware of the mistakes; and second, they were not impressed by them. Some went as far as to write additional comments, such as, 'You would make mistakes, wouldn't you? It's what we have come to expect of you.'

In a similar case, a database entry was once issued about my company that was riddled with mistakes. I had not made these mistakes: the copy I had provided was 100 per cent correct – but the company in charge of the database had inputted the copy incorrectly. They did not offer me a proof to check prior to issue. My regret was that I had not requested this; I assumed that they would send it. The result was that the company was not embarrassed by their mistake – but I certainly was. The carelessness, lack of quality and professionalism of the agency reflected more on my company than on them.

In a similar way, the transport provider had either not requested a proof of the final questionnaire or had not vetted it sufficiently before issue. They came to regret this oversight. Their admirable intentions were seriously undermined. This is why no organization can ever truly afford to outsource responsibility for their corporate writing.

If this is a demanding task even in your native market, imagine how much more demanding it is to get it right if your PR activities are in English as a foreign language. You need to make sure that someone in your company is accountable at every stage for checking accuracy and meaning when writing is outsourced.

Your checklist for action

■ Make your release as topical, interesting and newsworthy as possible.

■ Target the right publication and use English that is likely to engage its readers.

■ Make your release clear, correct and concise. There is nothing busy editors like better than interesting copy that is well written.

■ Remember to sell your message.

■ Tailor the format suggested in this chapter for your press release – and always provide a covering note to editors.

■ Take care that the timing of your publicity is right.

■ Avoid unintentional jokiness, especially in serious notices such as product recalls.

■ Jargon rarely works in press releases; use it only with great care – or not at all.

■ You cannot outsource accountability for accuracy of the English used and completeness of message.

9

Writing reports

The changing face of reports

Global companies do not always require staff to write formal reports in English. Often the reports of yesteryear have now been replaced by presentations, as I mentioned in Chapter 4. Or they have been replaced by business reviews and collaborative reports. These are where a writer gathers facts and adds their and possibly others' evaluation of these, as a business case for consideration. The review can be a question of creating an open dialogue, which may or may not lead to a conclusion in due course.

Whichever style your organization prefers, you will have a writing template to use. So my tips that follow are designed to help you plan your writing stages methodically.

Evaluate your target audience and your role

As far as you possibly can, identify before you write:

- Why are you writing and who will be your key readers?

- How much do they know? What is their proficiency in English?

- Do they need to use the report? If so, how? For example, to improve results in areas in which they are accountable? To be kept informed about others' achievements?

- Are they interested in the report or must you create that interest?

- What must you do in the report: inform, persuade, cover yourself, anticipate problems, offer solutions?

- Do you need to monitor any results and have an ongoing status record?

A checklist to help you plan

1. Take time to understand the brief. If it is in English make sure you fully understand what is written. Evaluate the business case.

2. Check the deadline.

3. Who, if anyone, has input alongside yours?

4. Check and set the relevant background.

5. Understand the target audience and how to write the right English for them.

6. What analysis is needed?

7. What recommendations should you or others make?

8. Draw up your plan for the report.

9. Write the report and evaluate how to make the right impact, distinguishing between:

   - essential to know;

   - nice to know;

   - do not need to know.

10. Check what you have written for both sense and logic.

11. Check your writing for mistakes in your English, including a spellcheck and grammar check in the correct variety of English.

12. Issue and check both the outcomes and the feedback after your audience has received your report or review. Did your English work?

Different perspectives

The constant theme throughout this book is that our writing is most effective when we address things as much from our readers' perspectives as from our own. In fact, problems arise when we do not.

You will have different guidelines for different reports. If you are required to take an audit, you will need to write objective communication that is fair, impartial and unbiased, and is the result of a balanced assessment of all relevant facts and circumstances. You can go further. You can shine through the way you write and be thanked by your readers (implicitly if not explicitly) for the signposts you provide.

In fact, it is probably true to say that business reports and reviews are mostly written for discussion, to make recommendations and to persuade. In those instances, readers are likely to want report writers to remember how busy they are. They may require only the essential details and may not need a step-by-step account of everything that happened, in the sequence in which it happened. Their view can be that it is the writer's job to highlight and prioritize the milestones and key messages in accessible English.

If you are the writer, bear this in mind and consider whether you should focus on:

- explaining what the report or review is about at the very outset;

- setting things in context to help your readers;

- using an appendix or appendices so that readers who need to access further information can do so. These readers may be those who are more proficient in English, for example, or who are more closely involved with the subject.

A major problem to avoid!

Once again, I cannot stress enough that any attachments must also be in English. Time after time, writers in global companies make a huge mistake here. Without thinking, non-native English writers might attach an appendix in their own language to their main report in English. This has an unfortunate result: they may alienate their target audience, who literally may not be able to understand them.

Case study

I regularly deliver 'How to write reports in English' courses to companies that operate globally. But very often I am given a training brief that even I find daunting in its dryness of expression. How can anybody ever get enthusiastic about writing reports in English on that basis?

It may surprise you to hear that sometimes companies have the answer under their own noses, so to speak. Over the years I have found gems on the following lines where report writers 'bring something to their writing' that can really help readers. Examples are:

'This review shows how we can reduce expenditure by £10,000 this year without reducing customer service.'

'In particular, these shortcomings mean that we cannot launch the project as planned.'

'Most importantly, your decision is needed on item 3.'

'We need to ask the HR department to increase/decrease the staffing arrangements for this quarter.'

'These figures comfortably exceed the target for the year.'

In each case the writing helps the reader see key points and the direction needed. Great business writing always leads readers where they need to be.

Add a personal note to add human interest

On a very positive note, I am always particularly impressed when writers use accessible English to add some personal note that adds human interest. Examples are:

'Congratulations to the team.'

'We all have an interest in keeping our customers happy. We would not be here without them.'

'This is just the start of our journey. Let's work together to reach our destination.'

It shows how no writing need ever appear inhuman or boring. Indeed, all writing should be eminently clear, however technical it is. If you are enthusiastic about what you write, it shows. Your readers can even share your enthusiasm. I know I have! I have read reports by my clients on shipping law, gas boilers, underwater cables, automotive parts, insurance, engineering plants, transportation, medical equipment ... to name just a few. And the best business writers share one thing in common. They make me interested in what they write and help me to gain understanding of why they do what they do.

Can you think of some expressions in accessible English that you could use in your reports to get people on board? Why not note some down now?

Making your mark and anticipating questions

In Chapter 3, I highlighted the importance of anticipating likely questions when you deliver a presentation. The same advice applies when you write reports. Otherwise people may feel that you are wasting their time – even if they do not say this to your face.

Anticipating questions – and asking them of yourself beforehand – is a particularly valuable approach when you write reports in English in which you know that certain items may be contentious or complex. Cover those points and you will be noticed by key people for all the right reasons, including:

■ for being systematic;

■ for thinking around the subject;

■ for making their life easier, whether they are native or non-native English speakers.

Writing can inadvertently put up barriers

You now know that large blocks of written text make readers not want to read, and that writing complicated sentences will not make you seem more intelligent. Combine the two and you are building your own barriers to effective writing.

Another barrier of a writer's own making can be overusing the passive voice in English writing. We have seen that the active voice is where the subject does the action. Sentences that show this are:

'The IT department is currently reviewing this issue.'

'The treasurer highlights the problems involved.'

The passive voice is where the subject of the active clause becomes secondary, where it is acted upon or receives the action. Often the word 'by' is added, as we can see in the following sentences:

'The issue is currently being reviewed by the IT department.'

'The problems involved are highlighted by the treasurer.'

In both these examples, we can still see who is doing the action. But sometimes the passive is used in reports without any reference to ownership – and then it can become problematic for readers to understand who does what (if anything). An example of a passive that can lead to uncertain outcomes is: 'This issue is currently being reviewed.'

The reader may be uncertain about who is carrying out the review. The context may indicate this, but often it does not. In any event, why make your reader have to refer too closely to context when your meaning can be crystal clear if you write the active form?

You will find more on use of active and passive in writing in the next Chapter.

The structure you design always matters, even in a report that essentially only describes facts. Every word should add value so that the reader knows, almost at a glance:

■   what the situation was or is;

■   who is responsible for getting it right;

■   who does what next and when.

Technical reports

In many cases, reports written by non-native English speakers will be at a technical level, and the standard of written English can vary enormously.

Case study

Cross-cultural technical reports in a multinational aviation company

A leading multinational aviation company knows first-hand how difficult it can be to write reports in English for discussion by technical staff from multi-cultural backgrounds.

The organization found they were wasting a significant amount of time when they issued quite narrow guidelines on how to write English in reports. Participants clearly had differing levels of proficiency in English and many were asking a lot of questions about meanings.

Some misunderstood the written English to the point of asking the wrong questions in meetings. Not everyone realized this – which led to some of the group regularly being puzzled by the direction the meeting was going. In technical areas this clearly matters.

Those who did pinpoint the problem posed the obvious question. How could they improve the effectiveness of reports in English? The solution they found was this. The fact that much of the writing relates to technical issues for which there is a common understanding regardless of language – namely 'how things work' – can often be expressed in non-verbal language such as drawings, mathematics and so on. Often a block diagram can replace an enormous amount of written text.

So they rewrote the guidelines for how to write company technical reports in English on these lines.

Have you come across this frequent complication in multi-lingual organizations? If so, another good idea can be to have face-to-face meetings at regular intervals. This can result in much greater understanding, compared with an 'arm's-length' written discussion in English as a second language.

A key feature of this book is to help you evaluate when writing in English is the best communication medium to drive your business forward – and when other modes need to be used in parallel.

Your checklist for action

■   If you do not actively highlight key messages and findings, do not assume that readers can identify them.

■   We write in business for business purposes and to market ourselves and our organization.

■   Every piece of business English writing we put out offers us potential to shine.

■   Improve the impact of reports by adopting a corporate style; make reports logical and seamless, to have the right impact.

■   Do not rely on cutting and pasting Word® documents in which different writers may have different styles of writing English.

■   Include a clear summary for busy readers, where you can.

■   Write concise English and construct reports with the busy executive in mind.

■   Try to use active rather than passive constructions.

■   Make sure that any attachments are also in English.

■   In short, design your reports using the key principles of this book: make impact rather than create barriers; understand when you need to persuade.

10

Writing agendas, meeting notes and minutes

Writing a meeting agenda

If you have to write an agenda, take the opportunity to design a good working model. Be aware that the agenda must:

- be specific to the meeting and results focused;
- prepare people for why the meeting is necessary;
- set the best order possible for items to appear;
- be clearly defined and well set out, taking house style into account;
- be circulated well in advance of the meeting.

Ideally, agree the agenda with the chairperson as far in advance of the meeting as possible. People need notice of the agenda and papers (usually a minimum of two or three working days), so you need to have all information available well before this.

Purpose and objectives in a typical agenda

The objectives are likely to be procedural formalities: discussing and taking key strategic decisions, reviewing operations, communication with other parties to inform or gain external input, considering and enabling successful succession planning throughout the organization, ensuring that the company implements all necessary procedural and compliance items across the range. So planning a good agenda presents you with the opportunity to manage a meeting's success before it even starts.

Your planning can be along the following lines:

- Purpose of meeting.

- Does the agenda support the purpose?

- Is it concise?

- Is it well structured, in the right running order? Has an alternative running order ever been considered, eg in which minutes are considered? Or action-oriented project meetings?

- Is pre-reading required? Do you indicate this? Do you enable this?

- Have contributors been alerted to prepare materials for circulation, and have they been given a deadline? Do they observe it? Could you do any more to help?

- Are the agenda and supporting papers always circulated on time?

It is an inescapable fact that many meetings take place without clarity or agreement about who contributes, when, and the contribution they need to make in the meeting itself. If the starting point is wrong, then the meeting is not on track to succeed from the outset.

Make an impact in meeting notes and minutes

People need to wake up to the often overlooked fact that minutes of meetings (or the notes of informal meetings) are not just about summarizing discussions and actions. As much about aiding management follow-up, they are an essential management tool. Indeed, skilled minute takers are very important to any organization.

So what more fundamental writing tips can I give here? From the outset, the best advice is to have a pre-meeting briefing with the chairperson of the meeting if this is at all possible. Forewarned is forearmed, which basically means: knowledge before the event equals power.

Do not be the person who is puzzled or left without the answers when it comes to writing the minutes in English and recording the follow-up after the meeting.

People often underestimate how important and challenging the role of minute taker is – especially in cross-cultural organizations, where everyone may not be using English in the same way. Sometimes you only have yourself to blame if, as a minute taker, you do not insist on being regarded as a co-manager of the meeting. It will help you so much if you do – and your minute writing will get so much easier as a result. You will have the confidence to ask when you are unsure of what is being said, or where a particular point is leading.

Write effective minutes by understanding the importance of:

■ working out style and format before the meeting if possible;

■ staying calm and confident;

■ concentrating not simply on every word spoken but on sorting the essential from the inessential aspects;

■ resisting personal interpretation;

■ asking questions to clarify things to ensure you get the whole picture (before the meeting moves on) – otherwise how can you write the right English?

■ questioning what technical terms mean if you are not sure, as you will have to write them;

■ asking questions (either yourself or via the chairperson) to make sure speakers understand the remit of the meeting – and that any problems are being solved. Once again, remember that it is you who will have to write the record in English.

Action sheets

In most organizations, meetings and minutes are usually action-oriented. Yet even when writing in their native language, both native English and non-native English minute takers may feel their work is complete if they record only an outline sketch of each action. This may be within the main minute and is often in passive form. The following example shows what I mean: 'It was decided that a report should be submitted to the next meeting.'

Does this writing exemplify best practice? I do not think so. Just recording actions is not the end of the story. The action is hidden. In English there are subtle differences in meaning between 'should' and 'must' or 'needs to be' and 'has to be'. 'Should' is more tentative than the other three options – and ownership can be lost. In that sentence above, who has to do the report ? Somebody or nobody?

In performance terms, it is not good enough. The minutes' storyline has to continue to make the right impact and to work. It should be about clearing actions and about recommendations (the things people need to go away and do, and when they must do this by). You are more likely to write great minutes (after what should be results-driven meetings) if you build action sheets alongside the narrative element.

Ditch the passive form and substitute the active form and concrete actions. Here is an example: 'The finance director needs to report on action 123 at the next meeting on 5 November.' You may also wish to record actions in a column on the right-hand side of the minutes; or write them on a separate page for subsequent circulation.

Style tips for minutes

One easy way of writing reader-friendly minutes with impact is simply to vary the vocabulary you use. Minutes should not be a boring, 'dead' record of something that took place at some point in time, though they so often are.

You may be able to make your mark here. Take the opportunity to look at your minute writing afresh. Minutes are a form of writing likely to impact not just on the present but on the future too. They are vital – so write them with vitality! Try to avoid the flat, lacklustre style of yesteryear and actively choose to write minutes that are attractively presented, interesting and easy to read. You are missing a trick if you do not.

Examples of different minute styles

You will see both the following styles when minutes are written in English. I know which I prefer.

Even though the second is slightly longer, the informative headings make it easier for readers (especially non-NE readers) to dip in and out of the text. Also, the English used is more reader-friendly and congratulatory to staff for jobs well done. This is an excellent way to build bridges in cross-cultural scenarios.

Director's quarterly report

The director congratulated everyone in the company for having achieved the Investors in People standard, saying that this is an achievement all employees should be proud of.

He provided the board with an update on the ABC order. As a contingency against any problems that could arise, company planners had worked hard to reallocate most of the deliveries to CDE by the end of the quarter.

The director noted that the final part of the XYZ project was launched on 15 March.

Director's quarterly report

Congratulations to all staff on achieving Investors in People standard

The director congratulated everyone in the company on the award of this prestigious standard, saying that this was an achievement all employees should be proud of.

Update on the ABC order

The director thanked company planners for working hard to reallocate most of the deliveries to CDE by the end of this quarter, thus preventing any problems arising.

Successful launch of XYZ Project

The director confirmed the successful launch of the final part of the XYZ project on 15 March.

Vocabulary tips

A thesaurus can be useful for this writing genre, though not if you misuse it by choosing the most obscure language. Used wisely it can be a very useful aid.

If, say, you are recording discussions, it can be helpful to alternate use of a word such as 'said' with different words to energize your text. You could try the many alternatives that exist in English, such as 'stated', 'discussed', 'proposed', 'reported', 'considered' and so on.

If something is 'decided' you could also use alternatives such as 'confirmed', 'approved', 'verified', 'resolved' and so on.

A meeting can have 'ended' and it could also have 'concluded', 'terminated' or 'finished'.

By varying vocabulary, you effectively make reading minutes less of a chore and more of a tool to get the right results out of each meeting. By getting into the habit of reducing words wherever possible, you soon streamline your writing.

For example, you could swap ...

'The director said the review would take six months and he concurred with a request that he would report back regarding this in due course'

... for the more streamlined version ...

'The review would take six months and the director agreed to report further to the next scheduled meeting after this.'

Not only does the revised sentence contain five fewer words, it is also time-bound: we know when the director will be reporting back (and this should be outlined in an action sheet issued with the minutes). The minutes are more concise and, equally importantly, lead somewhere. We know what happens next, who does it and when.

Defining timescales will help you

Many organizations have a rule that minutes must be not only written but also circulated within 48 hours. This may sound difficult but if it you can achieve it, do so. It is ultimately in everyone's interests, because the sooner we record discussions and decisions taken, the better our recall is. This is especially so if the English that was used is not our native language.

The best outline meeting notes in the world can make less sense when our attention is distracted by newer events and more recent discussions. Other people's memories fade too. If amendments have to be made (and this is all part of the minute-writing cycle) it is easier to get agreement on this sooner rather than later.

Converting notes to minutes: the vital stages

Know your house style and know whether you can adapt this before you convert your notes. This can be your opportunity to see whether changes can be made, as all writing styles need to be reviewed periodically, as businesses evolve.

Use a good layout to impress your readers before they even read the subject matter. Keep your readers in mind and judge how much they know of the topics in question – and how much they need to see in the minutes. Include references made to important specifics, such as:

- events, dates, locations;
- money and budgets;
- contracts;
- names of departments, people or outside bodies etc.

Use informative headings and paragraphs. If you use headings for new subjects and paragraphs for each new point made, people will know which items are of most relevance to them. This is the vital 'What's in it for me?' factor. You then enable them to read the minutes in bite-sized portions, so to speak, and maybe even out of sequence, because not everyone who reads minutes has to read every item. As long as everything is there, you have done your job.

For example, 'Completed launch of Project 1/2011' will make more impact and be easier for a reader to find than 'project 1/2011 launch'. If your busy manager just needs to check the status on that project they will thank you for highlighting it – and for the figurative 'pat on the back' you have expressed in writing.

Evaluate the words and format you use. Write as positively as possible. As you know by now, this entire book is about identifying personal and organizational values you need readers to see, so show these! If targets have been reached, that is great news, so why not use a heading that will highlight this? If there is any shortfall in performance this will have to be recorded. But there are always reasons, and there are usually solutions, so it helps if you can highlight these too in your minutes.

Review of minutes: handle with care

When you have to write minutes in English which non-native English speakers will review, it can be disheartening at times. Perfectly good English can be mistakenly 'corrected', sometimes wrongly, at the review stage by minute writers' non-native English managers or colleagues. I feel sorry for minute takers when this happens.

If it happens to you, my advice is this. You know that line managers can feel a need to revise writing of others, even the authors who are writing in their own language. Ultimately we may have to accept that we write to suit our line managers' preferences. After all, they are responsible overall for every piece of writing that goes out.

But it's also true to say that, if you work in a supportive working environment (and I hope you do), those making amendments should always explain why they are changing someone's writing. I see no reason why minute writers should not also feel confident to explain, politely and non-contentiously, why they chose the English they did. Their managers may see the light.

Your checklist for action

▪ Understand that agendas, meeting notes and minutes are a valuable management tool.

▪ Write them so that they tell a continuing story.

▪ Use active rather than passive constructions to help clarity.

▪ Indicate clearly in writing what happens next and who does it.

▪ Plan the meeting cycle and set clear timetables for contributions etc.

11

Word Power Skills 2.0

The concept of Web 2.0 is that the worldwide web is not one-way but interactive. Businesses need to understand how to put themselves in their customers' position. It seems to me that it would be very narrow-minded not to understand that this concept does not stop there. It applies absolutely to every aspect of interfacing with customers today.

As I have defined customers at the outset of this book as anyone with whom you have to deal, let's apply the concept of what I call written Word Power Skills 2.0 to creating interactive written content.

Plain English manuals and instructions

At an export trade function I happened to tell a delegate that I often help companies write their manuals in plain English.

'Wow!' he exclaimed. 'You could save the world by doing that!'

He went on to explain that what he meant was how much easier life would be in a world without confusing instructions and so-called guidelines that are actually undecipherable (whether or not English is your native language). After all, the whole point about instructions is that they are one of life's necessities: guidelines to help us conduct our daily life in some way. They are supposed to make life easier, not more difficult.

His reaction was so heartfelt that it made me realize we have a major problem here. How great it would be if this book can be an instrument of change, one that easily and cheaply improves the quality of its readers' lives.

Make a difference by demystifying instructions

Why do so many manuals in English mystify rather than demystify the topics they cover? Especially when their focus is people-centred subjects such as health and safety instructions, staff induction handbooks, pension arrangements, self-assembly furniture, to name just a few? Naturally some aspects of purely technical writing are always going to be unintelligible to the casual reader.

But it is not this specialist writing that frustrates people. Frustration sets in when the lay person, the end-user, has to interface with the writing and finds an impenetrable or quasi-impenetrable screen of words. And this is exactly my point. Do you understand what 'quasi-impenetrable' means? Many of you will, but many of you will not. It would be better if I referred to a screen of words that are 'almost impossible to understand'. More readers are likely to understand this plainer English – and that matters in business.

Let's start with the simplest instructions – for example, on how to make coffee in the office. Why not make it people-centred and appealing from the start? For example, why not write 'How to make the perfect cup of coffee' rather than 'Instructions regarding making of coffee'? It sounds obvious, yet sometimes people have to be encouraged to write this way. Once they know they can, they can be so pleased about this, and so are their readers.

Using double negatives in English can lead to confusion – and nowhere more so than in instructions. Even native English speakers have to take time to read this double-negative construction: 'Using components that have not been manufactured on site is not permitted.' It is much easier to read and understand the same message expressed positively as: 'You must use components that have been manufactured on site.'

There can also be nuances of meaning (subtle differences in meaning) in the following double negative: 'It's not imposs-ible.' This could mean: 'It is possible' or 'It is possible but is probably difficult to achieve.' Another example can be: 'I can't not do it' which actually means 'I must do it' rather than 'I can do it' as you might expect.

Writing for people or for processes?

This is a question that we should regularly ask ourselves. We tend to write opaque instructions when we focus on processes rather than the people who have to follow the instructions. It can be yet another area where we find the negative influence of 'passive' English writing.

Let's look at a business case to illustrate this. A customer is experiencing problems with their insurance company and has told their insurance broker. Look at two different approaches that the broker could take when writing in reply to them:

Approach 1: 'Necessary steps are being taken in connection with the relevant documentation and it is to be hoped that these are now in order; your point about overpayments to the insurance company has been noted and, in addition, processes regarding policy renewals are being implemented as appropriate.'

Approach 2: 'I trust that you will find everything to be in order but I will phone on Tuesday to ensure that all policies will be renewed on the correct basis. With regard to the overpayments that you feel you have been making to your insurers, if you let me have the reference number noted on the bank statement and the amount that was being collected each month, I will make the necessary enquiries to resolve the matter.'

You can see the differences in style. Which do you think the customer will prefer?

Because approach 1 is slightly shorter, we might say it must be better as it is more concise. On the other hand, writing in English, whether for a home or global audience, is not necessarily just about cutting words out. Economy of words can be good – but not at the expense of editing out words that add value. Very often the best business English writing is concise but it also has the right tone. So ultimately, although approach 1 is shorter, its overall message is less effective – because it is less clear and, crucially, it is not reader-friendly.

Let me help you analyse the styles used in approaches 1 and 2, so that you can see this for yourself. Let's first look at approach 1:

- Does the writing tell you that something is being done to help the customer in view of their feedback?

- If so, who is doing something to help?

- Is there anything in the writing to give the customer confidence that something is actively being done?

■ Is the writing time-bound: does the customer know what will happen next and when?

I think you will find that your answers in relation to approach 1 are likely to be 'no'. Now let's ask the same questions regarding approach 2. Here your answers are more likely to be 'yes'. Clearly the different writing styles give rise to differing reader reactions. Why should this be?

It is probably because approach 1 uses passive English writing. The subject is hidden and the overall feel of the writing is that something may or may not happen to resolve the situation. The customer has no reassurance on this and there is nothing expressed that will make the customer feel valued.

In contrast, approach 2 uses active writing, referring to 'I' and 'you'. The writer is taking accountability: they are dealing with the problem on the customer's behalf. What's more, they are giving a time frame in which this is going to happen. It gives the reader confidence that there will be a successful outcome. Bearing in mind that the subject matter is insurance – which clearly matters to the customer – the writer is also giving the customer added peace of mind.

If we can achieve this through well-designed, totally sincere writing, let's go for it! Besides, the great news is that word power skills – of which this is a prime example – are a virtually free resource. Any individual and any business large or small, anywhere in the world, can harness them right away.

More on how to improve impact in instructions

Here are two notices, both based on a real-life example of a notice that really was issued to staff in an organization. See how differently they work.

Company notice: to be issued to all staff

INCIDENCE OF SPELLING AND GRAMMAR ERRORS
IN BUSINESS WRITING

A fact has been noticed over recent years that an
increase in mistakes in business writing have become
an increasingly significant problem apparently in view
of the fact that, with increased computer usage and an
absence at the present time of traditional secretaries,
more business writing is being undertaken than was
previously the case.

It has in addition been noted that e-mails and files
attached thereto sent by users that are seen to have errors
can cause negative reactions for receivers.

Any of several programs can be used to check whether
errors have been made and it has been noted that either
grammar or spelling mistakes have been involved. The
program used by this organization may be obtained
by users from the supplies team manager within the IT
department. Even where no problems have been noticed
in this connection, spelling and grammar should be
checked for frequently where there is an exchange of
information with other users.

Writing tip to help all colleagues: please read now

Checking for spelling and grammar errors when you
write

Readers say they see more mistakes in business writing
today. The problem may arise from the sharp rise in

businesses using computers, alongside the fact there are fewer traditional secretaries. These developments mean that more people have to write their own business correspondence.

We know that readers (who can be either internal or external customers) can be irritated by mistakes in e-mails and files we send.

To help us all get things right, here are some tips to help:

- If the program we are supposed to use is not yet installed on your computer, please contact John Smith, Supplies Manager, in our IT department (contact details) who will help.

- Even if you have not noticed any problems, please always check spelling and grammar before you send e-mails and files.

The second version uses far fewer words – 148 compared with 174 – but adds more value. Why? Because it is a document that people can understand and own. They know what they must do and who can help. They also know why it matters if they make mistakes – not because they are naughty schoolchildren but because readers (who, crucially, are customers) may not like it. The second version yields a positive business result. Also, if we can save some 20-plus words in each instruction piece of writing, it quickly adds up. Editing to ensure clear, concise writing soon becomes second nature. You have the very satisfying ability to prove that less really can be more.

Websites: words are everything in cyberspace

Because English is the predominant language of the web, use your written English to make your messages, products or services stand out in the right way. Attract readers' attention for the right reasons and use accessible English to write the steps they can follow.

Search engine optimization: advertising your website

Search engine optimization is the name given to improving a website's ranking to enhance the likelihood of visitors finding it when they search the internet. Choosing the right keywords is crucial to success here, as is writing information-rich material for the site.

So if you are writing your content in English, this is one more reason to simplify the language you use. Why? Because the words people type in for a search are generally the simplest ones. So you could particularly focus on Step 4 in the writing system that I show in Chapter 7. Use as your keywords the words people are likely to type when looking for the products or services you provide. Identify the most obvious descriptive words in English and include these on the pages on your site. For example, if you provide security systems you may find people type 'burglar alarms' or 'light sensors' rather than the generic wording 'security systems'. Or if you train staff at contact centres, people who require your services may type 'spoken skills' rather than 'training for contact centre staff'.

Website processes, visuals and content

In the early days of websites, many businesses gave priority to processes and visuals over copy (the writing). Probably for this reason, companies often left their website development largely to IT and design specialists. It meant that, in many cases, these professionals would simply slot in standard marketing copy in English, supplied either by their own copywriters (sometimes hired on a when-needed basis) or by their client company, even when using English that they were not entirely proficient in.

Enlightened companies saw there could be a problem here. Internet users visit websites to gain information. Usually they gain it through written words; and they expect to find the answers they need at the click of an on-screen button. Processes and visuals certainly matter, but users will not click on a button if the words they want to see (in this context, the English that relates well to their needs) are not there.

Everything on a website must align

In Chapter 4, I mentioned how the pictures and captions used in advertising material should align, and mentioned examples where this is not always the case. Sometimes you will find that pictures and words do not join up correctly in websites too. They lose the right impact as a result.

We do not write websites for ourselves: they are for our audience, our target market. The moment a website says the wrong thing, or confuses in any way, can be the moment an internet user decides to exit a site. We have all done it. Simply mismatching the wrong written English caption with the wrong picture may puzzle people, and the drift of our message or pitch is thrown off course.

In other instances, the caption is correctly aligned with a picture but is poorly written. Maybe the English is incorrect

– which is bad news, as readers tend to focus on captions. Or the caption may detract from the picture because its message is not right. For instance, on one website I saw a picture of a personable young man with an obviously feminine name (let's say Anna) and on the next page was a picture of a personable young woman with an obviously male name (let's say Robert). This may be faintly amusing, but readers may think 'If they cannot get that right, what *will* they get right?'

Forums: the power of a deluge of written responses

Cyberspace is full of people passionate about exercising freedom of speech and about putting over their point of view. Are you active in forums? If not, the chances are increasing daily that you will be. If you do visit forums you may have seen amazingly long forum threads. Indeed, a thread of over 1,000 comments is not unheard of. It can happen that such an unwieldy thread is the direct result of the originator of the discussion making some mistake in the first e-mail discussion sent. It can be the nature of the medium that just one wrongly crafted message can have the effect of creating the exact opposite meaning to the one originally intended. This can lead to a deluge of almost instant written replies.

So what does this tell us? It clearly demonstrates that it is now more important than ever to get our writing right. If you had been reading a business book 10 years ago, you would probably not have been so ready to comment in writing (whether to criticize or praise) as you are likely to be today. The barrage of responses to all matters, great and small, demonstrates this all too well.

The immediacy of written responses by e-mail can catch organizations out. Let's take a recent case affecting the BBC, the

UK television broadcaster. Two well-known radio presenters left some unguarded remarks on an actor's telephone answering machine. They thought their comments were amusing and harmless in intent. They then relayed their messages live on national radio. The actor found the comments tasteless. He complained – and he was not alone. The BBC was inundated with thousands of complaints from members of the public who were offended by the presenters' remarks. The minority of those who complained were those who had actually heard the live broadcast. The majority had only heard about the broadcast, checked it out for themselves, and then e-mailed their complaints.

In the past, when people complained, they had to take the time and make the effort to write a letter and pay for the postage to send it. It took some effort to do this. Nowadays, with the internet at our disposal, we can each e-mail a complaint in very little time, with little effort and at little cost. So the BBC found itself having to react very quickly. It had to make a public announcement on this issue long before any inquiry could publish its findings.

That is the immediate impact the written word can now have. As another example, amateur film critics' blogs can have a significant and rapid effect on the success or failure of new films. Indeed, the most-read blogs have the power to impact on companies in a way that would never even have been imagined just some years back.

Writing e-mails to make an impact

This book is about writing English with impact. But you will never make the right impact with your e-mails if your recipients feel you are littering their inbox and, by implication, wasting their time. On the other hand, you will greatly improve your chances of making the right impact if you view every e-mail you send out as:

■ a personal and company advertisement (which means you will not want to put your reputation on the line);

■ a piece of writing that you have designed to get the results you need;

■ something you know will highlight your professionalism;

■ something you are happy that other people (not just your intended recipients) may see.

Your checklist for action

■ Write English for people, not processes.

■ Use active rather than passive constructions in manuals, instructions etc.

■ Get your words in English right (on every level) on websites; in the final analysis, words are the site's most important feature.

■ Remember to update your words and your writing style in English regularly.

■ Think carefully before you send an e-mail or post anything online.

■ Be aware of how quickly your mistakes will be written about on blogs – so try to make sure you do not feature in blogs for the wrong reasons.

Conclusion

By now you should be feeling very motivated to make the right impact and get yourself and your organization noticed – for all the right reasons.

You will have closed the skills gap of where you were before you read the book, to where you are now and to where you want to be. The good news is that writing English for business is a key and – this is crucially important – highly transferable skill. Carry on closing the gap and see how many opportunities you will create for yourself. Take these tips on board, so that everything you write from now on is likely to be good – and you will actually keep on getting better. Congratulations on this.

Don't hold yourself back. Why set limits? You have got the power here: written word power skills.

As you will have seen, the Preface to this book explains how the series fits together, to offer you a comprehensive and invaluable reference guide for almost all aspects of your business English writing needs.

The sharpest minds
need the finest advice

visit
www.koganpage.com
today